# CONSTRUCTION (DESIGN AND MANAGEMENT) REGULATIONS 1994

AUSTRALIA
LBC Information Services
Sydney


CANADA and U.S.A.
Carswell
Toronto ● Ontario


NEW ZEALAND
Brooker's
Auckland


SINGAPORE and MALAYSIA
Thomson Information (S.E. Asia)
Singapore

# CONSTRUCTION (DESIGN AND MANAGEMENT) REGULATIONS 1994

by

David J. Henderson, LL.B (Hons); ACI Arb.,
Solicitor
(MacRoberts, Glasgow)
and
Gareth R. Parry, BA (Hons)., Solicitor
(MacRoberts, Glasgow)

LONDON
SWEET & MAXWELL
1996

Published in 1996 by
Sweet & Maxwell Limited of
100 Avenue Road
Swiss Cottage
London, NW3 3PF


Typeset by Mendip Communications Ltd, Frome, Somerset

Printed in the United Kingdom by
Headway Press, Reading.


No natural forests were destroyed to make this product:
only farmed timber was produced and replanted


ISBN 0421 574402


**A CIP catalogue record for this book is available
from the British Library**

# PREFACE

This book provides a commentary on the Construction (Design and Management) Regulations 1994 and highlights the strengths, weaknesses and, in a few cases, the ambiguities in the Regulations.

The Regulations are the Health and Safety Commission's first steps in an overhaul of health and safety law in the construction industry, and were drafted against a background of increasing numbers of accidents in the industry. For the first time a system of responsibility for health and safety both on site and off has been introduced, with important new duties being placed on employers or promoters of projects and on those involved in the design and construction processes.

In preparing this book we have tried to anticipate and answer the inevitable practical problems of those whose work will be affected by the Regulations, including clients, designers, contractors, planning supervisors and other property professionals. Nevertheless, this book should be read in conjunction with the guidance notes and the Approved Code of Practice published by the Health and Safety Commission.

We should like to thank our colleague Craig Turnbull for his invaluable help in the research and preparation of this book.

The law is stated as at March 1, 1996.

*David Henderson*
*Gareth Parry*

v

# CONTENTS

PARA.

CONTENTS

# TABLE OF CASES

# TABLE OF E.C. LEGISLATION

# GLOSSARY

Extracted from HSC "Guide to managing health and safety in construction"

**Client:** Clients are those who are involved in a trade, business or other undertaking (whether for profit or not) and for whom construction work is carried out.

**Contractor:** Contractors include subcontractors and may also be known as works, specialist trade or nominated contractors. They have health and safety responsibilities for their own employees and others.

**Design:** Design is a wide term and includes specification and the production of drawings, design details and bills of quantity.

**Designers:** Designers are the organisations or individuals who carry out the design of the project. Designers may include architects, consulting engineers, quantity surveyors, specifiers, principal contractors and specialist subcontractors.

**Health and safety file:** This is a record of information for the client which focuses on health and safety. It alerts those who are responsible for the structure and equipment in it of the significant health and safety risks that will need to be dealt with during subsequent use, construction, maintenance, repair and cleaning work.

**Health and safety plan:** The health and safety plan serves two purposes. The pre-tender stage health and safety plan prepared before the tendering process brings together the health and safety information obtained from the client and designers and aids selection of the principal contractor. The health and safety plan during the construction phase details how the construction work will be managed to ensure health and safety.

**Notifiable:** Construction work is notifiable if it lasts longer than 30 days or will involve more than 500 person days of work.

**Planning supervisor:** The planning supervisor is a company, partnership, organisation or an individual who co-ordinates and manages the health and safety aspects of design. The planning supervisor also has to ensure that the pre-tender stage of the health and safety plan and the health and safety file are prepared.

**Principal contractor:**   This is the contractor appointed by the client who has the overall responsibility for the management of site operations. This includes the overall co-ordination of site health and safety management.

## 1994 No. 3140

## HEALTH AND SAFETY

### The Construction (Design and Management) Regulations 1994

|  |  |
|---|---|
| *Made* | *19th December 1994* |
| *Laid before Parliament* | *10th January 1995* |
| *Coming into force* | *31st March 1995* |

Arrangement of Regulations                                          **1.01**

1

Whereas the Health and Safety Commission has submitted to the Secretary of State, under section 11(2)(d) of the Health and Safety at Work etc. Act 1974**(a)** ("the 1974 Act"), proposals for the purpose of making regulations after the carrying out by the said Commission of consultations in accordance with section 50(3) of the 1974 Act;

And whereas the Secretary of State has made modifications to the said proposals under section 50(1) of the 1974 Act and has consulted the said Commission thereon in accordance with section 50(2) of that Act;

Now therefore, the Secretary of State, in exercise of the powers conferred on him by sections 15(1), (2), (3)(a) and (c), (4)(a), (6)(b) and (9), and 82(3)(a) of, and paragraphs 1(1)(c), 6(1), 14, 15(1), 20 and 21 of Schedule 3 to, the 1974 Act, and of all other powers enabling him in that behalf and for the purpose of giving effect to the said proposals of the said Commission with modifications as aforesaid, hereby makes the following Regulations:

## INTRODUCTION AND GENERAL NOTE

**1.02**    The Construction (Design and Management) Regulations 1994 (the "Regulations") were made under the Health and Safety at Work etc. Act 1974, s.15 and implement the design and management aspects of the Temporary or Mobile Construction Sites Directive (92/57: [1992] O.J. L.245/6) (see App. 1, below).

**1.03**    The Sites Directive lays down minimum health and safety requirements for temporary or mobile construction sites and seeks to raise the standard of construction health and safety management by improving co-ordination between the various parties at both the preparation stage of a construction project and its execution. The Regulations implement these aims by placing certain health and safety duties on clients, designers and contractors and by introducing new entities in the form of the planning supervisor and the principal contractor. The Regulations do not displace the general principles of prevention and protection as regards health and safety, nor do they displace the Management of Health and Safety at Work Regulations 1992 (S.I. 1992 No. 2051) requiring employers and the self-employed to make and maintain suitable and efficient risk assessments.

### European origins of the Regulations

#### *Treaty of Rome*
**1.04**    The origins of the Regulations may be found in Art. 118A of the Treaty establishing the European Economic Community (the Treaty of Rome), as amended in 1987 by the Single European Act. Art. 118A provides for closer co-operation by Community partners in, amongst other areas, the prevention of occupational accidents and diseases. The drafting of this Article was the subject of considerable

---

**(a)**    1974 c.37; sections 15 and 50 were amended by the Employment Protection Act 1975 (c. 71), Schedule 15, paragraphs 6 and 16 respectively.

political controversy amongst Member States, and provides that the European Council should adopt, by way of directives, certain minimum requirements regarding health and safety and should "*pay particular attention to encouraging improvements, especially in the working environment, as regards the health and safety of workers*". Art. 118A also requires that such directives are to avoid imposing administrative, financial and legal constraints which might hold back the creation and development of small and medium-sized undertakings.

### Framework Directive

The first directive to be issued under Art. 118A was the Framework Directive **1.05** (Council Directive 89/391: [1989] O.J. L.183/1) on the introduction of measures to encourage improvements in the safety and health of workers at work) under Art. 16 of which the European Council was to adopt individual directives dealing with, *inter alia*, (1) health and safety requirements for the workplace; (2) health and safety requirements for the use of work equipment for workers at work; (3) the use of personal protective equipment; (4) the manual handling of loads where there is a risk to workers; (5) health and safety requirements for work with display screen equipment; and (6) health and safety on temporary or mobile construction sites. The Sites Directive is the eighth individual directive to be implemented under the Framework Directive, Art. 16, the others being: Workplace Directive (Council Directive 89/655 ([1989] O.J. L.393/13) concerning the minimum safety and health requirements for the use of work equipment by workers at work); Use of personal protective equipment Directive (Council Directive 89/656 ([1989] O.J. L.393/18) on the minimum health and safety requirements for the use by workers of personal protective equipment at the workplace); Manual handling of loads Directive (Council Directive 90/269 ([1990] O.J. L.156/9) on the minimum health and safety requirements for the manual handling of loads where there is a risk particularly of back injury to workers); Display screen equipment Directive (Council Directive 90/270 ([1990] O.J. L.156/14) on the minimum safety and health requirements for work with display screen equipment); Carcinogens Directive (Council Directive 90/394 ([1990] O.J. L.196/1) on the protection of workers from the risks related to exposure to carcinogens at work); Biological agents Directive (Council Directive 90/679 ([1990] O.J. L.374/1) on the protection of workers from risks related to exposure to biological agents at work); and the Temporary Workers Directive (Council Directive 91/383 ([1991] O.J. L.206/19)). The Framework Directive is implemented in Great Britain by the Management of Health and Safety at Work Regulations 1992 and its Approved Code of Practice.

### Sites Directive

The Sites Directive (see App. 1, below) was published on August 26, 1992 **1.06** following protracted negotiations and discussions amongst Member States. Initial drafts of the Sites Directive favoured a rigid management approach and detailed annexes to the early drafts addressed, in considerable detail, specific hazardous aspects of construction work. One aspect of the rigid management approach proposed by the Commission included the appointment of a "manager" on site with ultimate responsibility for site safety. It was felt that the U.K. construction industry would be better served by adopting a more flexible approach, primarily by the appointment of a co-ordinator for health and safety. Following a consultation period, and the receipt of an Opinion from the European Parliament, the Commission's original proposals were amended, resulting in (1) a more restrictive definition of the exclusion of extractive industries, (2) an agreement that directors and other senior personnel of undertakings would remain liable for criminal prosecution notwithstanding the appointment of co-ordinators for the planning and implementation stages of a construction project, and (3) the adoption of the more flexible "co-ordination" role. The implementation of the Sites Directive was achieved on December 31, 1993.

**1.07**     The Sites Directive supplements and extends, but does not replace, the Framework Directive.

### Introduction and commencement of the Regulations

#### *Harmonising Safety Legislation*

**1.08**     The moves during the late 1980s and early 1990s by the European Commission, under Art. 118A, to harmonise health and safety legislation, which culminated with the Sites Directive, coincided with a rise in the number of accidents in the U.K. on construction sites. It is perhaps interesting to note that as far back as 1987 the Construction Industry Advisory Committee published guidelines which included amongst its advice on shortlisting contractors, the recommendations that: (1) health and safety factors should be considered when judging whether or not to invite a contractor to tender; and (2) technical and managerial competence should also be considered. In September 1989, as a result of increased concern at the rise in the number of construction site accidents, the Health and Safety Commission published a consultation document entitled "Construction Management—proposals for Regulations and an Approved Code of Practice" (a document which was influential in the approach adopted by the Commission in the Sites Directive). The Health and Safety Commission expressed the belief that the increase in the number of accidents on site could be attributed to the growth in sub-contracting, a diffusion of responsibility on site for health and safety and an increase in self-employment among building workers. Whilst those three observations are undoubtedly true, as applied to the late 1980s and early 1990s, they do not of themselves explain why the fragmentation of construction employment led to an increase in the number of on-site accidents. Whilst a detailed examination of these issues is beyond the scope of this commentary, two possible causal links appear feasible: (a) that the co-ordination of work on site is complex, given the number of parties on site at any one time and accordingly main contractors may have had difficulty in enforcing both their health and safety regulations and their common law duties to co-ordinate; and/or (b) that the financial pressures and constraints involved in tendering for contracting work in the late 1980s and early 1990s may have encouraged bidders to cut margins and, in particular, perceived soft areas such as health and safety matters.

#### *Focusing on Penalties*

**1.09**     The late 1980s also saw an increased focus on penalties for those responsible for health and safety accidents, culminating with the decision in January 1989 that penalties in England and Wales for breaches of regulations enforceable under the Health and Safety at Work etc. Act 1974 were to be increased, although the Government continued to resist the demands from some sectors, including Europe, for the penalties to include prison sentences for directors and/or senior managers of employers found guilty of breaches of the regulations—though see the note on criminal implications of the Regulations (paras. 1.21–1.28, below). Despite the increase in penalty levels, as reported in *Building* (February 23, 1990), the average fine for breach of health and safety regulations was £450, and the Government again urged the courts to "get tough" with building contractors found guilty of violating health and safety regulations.

#### *HSC Proposals*

**1.10**     In October 1992 the Health and Safety Commission, following consultation with the Health and Safety Commission's Construction Industry Advisory Committee (CONIAC), unveiled, for consultation, its draft regulations and approved code of practice to implement the design and management aspects of the Sites Directive. In the consultation document the Health and Safety Commission stated that its aims in implementing the Directive were fourfold:

"to avoid disrupting the basic framework established by the Health and Safety at Work etc. Act 1974, and also minimising change to the most recent regulations; to continue where appropriate the modernisation of health and safety law made prior to 1974, and to take the opportunity to repeal outdated UK legislation; to further the HSC/E philosophy of introducing control measures appropriate to the risk; [and] to propose regulations which meet the directives, but which generally do not go beyond them, so as to minimise the impact of alterations in the law at a time when the requirements of the EC necessarily mean considerable changes in the law. Nevertheless, the HSC proposes, where appropriate, to apply the directives to the self-employed and to public safety in conformity with the approach adopted in the HSW Act and subsequent regulations. In the case of the [Sites Directive], it has been necessary to extend the proposed regulations beyond the Directive to ensure that everyone who can contribute to improving health and safety in the industry is covered by the regulations."

In addition the consultation document notes that the principal aim of the Sites Directive is to *"raise the standard of construction health and safety management across the Community by improving co-ordination between the various parties involved at the preparation stage of a construction project and also when the work is being carried out ...".*

**1.11** During the consultation period concern was expressed, perhaps unsurprisingly by those likely to be undertaking additional roles, as to the costs of implementing the Regulations (including the potential for increased insurance premiums) and the lack of guidance for assessing competence. The Regulations were eventually scheduled for introduction on October 1, 1994 (having originally being scheduled for implementation on January 1, 1994) despite protests from a number of construction industry bodies including the Architects Council of Europe who urged the Commission to reconsider the Sites Directive and to delay implementation of the Regulations for 12 months. Following publication of the proposed Regulations, which included detailed transitional provisions for the phased introduction of the Regulations, an editorial in *Building* (April 29, 1994) contended that whilst it was hard to argue against the purpose of the Regulations, three fundamental flaws existed, namely (1) over-complex transitional arrangements; (2) lack of clarity as to what was intended to be covered by the Regulations; and (3) the danger that they would be paid no more than lip service. It suggested that *"... in three years, [the Regulations] will have become just another layer of irritating bureaucracy for the vast majority—more observed in the breach."* As the date for implementation drew nearer, concerns began to be expressed at the estimated costs of introducing and implementing the Regulations. Whilst the initial consultation paper had estimated potential costs of £550 million coupled with annual savings of £220 million, concern centred on the costs to small clients of appointing and training planning supervisors. The October 1, 1994 date was eventually put back to March 31, 1995, following moves to amend the Regulations and introduce certain threshold levels beneath which the Regulations would not apply in their entirety.

### Implementation of the Sites Directive by the Regulations

**1.12** The Regulations only implement the design and management aspects of the Sites Directive. Other provisions of the Sites Directive are to be implemented through other regulations. In particular the Sites Directive, Art. 10 (which extends certain of the Sites Directive duties to self-employed persons working on construction sites) is to be implemented as follows:

— the first parts of Art. 10.1(a)(i) and Art. 10.2(a)(i) are being implemented by the Management of Health and Safety at Work Regulations 1992;
— Art. 10.1(a)(ii) and Art. 10.2(a)(ii) are being implemented by the Provision and Use of Work Equipment Regulations 1992 (S.I. 1992 No. 2932) where they have not already been implemented by earlier regulations;
— Art. 10.1(a)(iii) and Art. 10.2(a)(iii) are being implemented by the Use of Personal Protective Equipment Regulations 1992 (S.I. 1992 No. 2966).

**1.13**     The remainder of the Sites Directive has been treated by the Health and Safety Commission in two parts. Pt. 1 deals with design and management, includes Arts. 1–7, 11–15, Annexes I–III, and those parts of Arts. 8–10 not dealt with elsewhere, and is implemented by the Regulations. Pt. 2 aims to apply to construction sites appropriate equivalent standards to those in the Workplace Directive, includes Annex IV and parts of Arts. 8 and 9, and is to be introduced through other legislation.

**Use of the Approved Code of Practice**

*Authority for Codes*

**1.14**     Under the Health and Safety at Work etc. Act 1974, s.16, the Health and Safety Commission may, with the approval of the Secretary of State and after consultation, approve and issue codes of practice for the purpose of providing practical guidance on the requirements of any provisions of the 1974 Act, ss.2–9, or the requirements of health and safety regulations made under *inter alia* the 1974 Act, s.15, of which the Regulations are an example. As the Approved Code of Practice states, it:

> "gives practical guidance with respect to the Construction (Design and Management) Regulations 1994, sections 2, 3 and 6 of the Health and Safety at Work etc. Act 1974, the Management of Health and Safety at Work Regulations 1992, and the Provision and Use of Work Equipment Regulations 1992."

**1.15**     The Approved Code of Practice (entitled "Managing construction for health and safety") in respect of the Regulations gained the "approved" status on January 3, 1995 and, together with the Regulations, came into effect on March 31, 1995.

*The Code and Civil Proceedings*

**1.16**     By virtue of the 1974 Act, s.17, a failure on the part of any person to observe the provisions of any approved code of practice does not of itself render him liable to any civil proceedings.

**1.17**     The question of applying the Approved Code of Practice in common law negligence cases is dealt with below (see General Note to reg. 21 (paras. 21.02–21.11, below). Although compliance with an approved code of practice may be of evidential value in civil proceedings, there is no presumption that such compliance equates to meeting the requisite standard of care at common law: see *Bux v. Slough Metals Ltd* [1974] 1 All E.R. 262. The Approved Code of Practice may, however, in time be regarded by the courts as establishing a certain standard against which any breach of duty of care may be judged.

*The Code and Criminal Proceedings*

**1.18**     A party's failure to observe a provision of the Approved Code of Practice does not *per se* render that party liable to criminal conviction. The 1974 Act, s.17, does, however, provide that where it is alleged that a party has committed an offence by virtue of a contravention of any requirement or prohibition imposed by or under any such provision as is mentioned in the 1974 Act, s.16(1), being a provision for which there is an Approved Code of Practice at the time of the alleged offence, then the

provisions of the 1974 Act, s.16(2), apply in relation to that Approved (
Practice. The 1974 Act, s.16(2), provides that if a provision of the Approved
Practice appears to the court to be relevant to the requirement or prohibition
to have been contravened it shall be admissible in evidence. This point is made in the
preface to the Approved Code of Practice which states:

> "This Code has been approved by the Health and Safety Commission and gives
> advice on how to comply with the law. This Code has a special legal status. If you
> are prosecuted for breach of health and safety law, and it is proved that you have
> not followed the relevant provisions of the Code, a court will find you at fault,
> unless you can show that you have complied with the law in some other way."

Further, if it is established that there was a failure to observe any provision of the **1.19**
Approved Code of Practice which appears to the court to be relevant to any matter
which it is necessary for the prosecution to prove in order to establish a contravention
of that requirement or prohibition, that matter shall be taken as proved unless the
court is satisfied that the requirement or prohibition was, in respect of that matter,
complied with otherwise than by way of observance of that provision of the
Approved Code of Practice.

In effect, if a person is shown not to have complied with the terms of the Approved **1.20**
Code of Practice, he is guilty of the offence unless the court is satisfied that the
requirement or prohibition is capable of being, and has been, complied with in a
manner other than that set out in the Approved Code of Practice. The onus of proof
is thus inverted. See *West Cumberland By Products Ltd v. D.P.P.* [1988] R.T.R. 391.

### Criminal implications of the Regulations

The 1974 Act, s.33(1)(c), provides that it is an offence for a person to contravene **1.21**
any health and safety regulations or any requirement or prohibition under any such
regulations.

A person guilty of a contravention of the 1974 Act, s.33(1)(c) is liable on summary **1.22**
conviction to a fine not exceeding £5,000 and on conviction on indictment to an
unlimited fine.

The 1974 Act, s.36, provides that where the commission by any person of an **1.23**
offence under any of the relevant statutory provisions is due to the act or default of
some other person, that other person shall be guilty of the offence. Proceedings in
such circumstances can be brought solely against the person whose act or default has
caused the offence, and need not be brought against the person who committed the
act or default.

The Interpretation Act 1978, s.5 and Sched. 1, provides that where a statute **1.24**
declares that the act or default of a person is an offence, such an offence applies
equally to bodies corporate.

The 1974 Act, s.37, provides that where an offence under any of the relevant **1.25**
statutory provisions is committed by a body corporate and it is proved to have been
committed with the consent and connivance of, or to have been attributable to any
neglect on the part of, any director, manager, secretary or other similar officer of the
body corporate or a person purporting to act in such a capacity, that person shall, in
addition to the body corporate, be guilty of an offence. In *Armour v. Skeen* 1977 J.C.
15, the then Director of Roads for Strathclyde Regional Council was convicted under
the 1974 Act, s.37(1) following the death of a council employee involved in bridge
repainting works. There are surprisingly few decisions on s.37, see *R. v. Mara* [1987]

1 All E.R. 478 and *Wotherspoon v. H.M.A.* 1978 J.C. 74. It appears that only those managers who have the power and responsibility to decide corporate policy and strategy are capable of being prosecuted, see *R. v. Boal* [1992] Q.B. 591, a case decided upon the Fire Precautions Act 1971 and *Woodhouse v. Walsall Metropolitan Borough Council* [1994] 1 B.C.L.C. 435, a case under the Control of Pollution Act 1974. Responsibility for the day-to-day running of a concern will not, of itself, be sufficient to expose an individual to conviction under s.37.

**1.26**   Where an emergency situation arises, and specialist advice is taken and complied with, it is likely that a court will conclude that it was not in the circumstances reasonably practicable to do anything more than comply with the advice received: see *Tudhope v. City of Glasgow District Council* 1986 S.C.C.R. 168.

**1.27**   As the Regulations are a "relevant statutory provision" for the purposes of the 1974 Act, s.21, if an inspector appointed under the 1974 Act, s.19, is of the opinion that a provision of the Regulations is being contravened in circumstances that make it likely that the contravention will continue or be repeated, he is empowered to serve an improvement notice. Further, where activities are being carried on that fall within the ambit of the Regulations and, in the opinion of the inspector, those activities involve or will involve a risk of serious personal injury, he may serve a prohibition notice. A detailed examination of improvement and prohibition notices is beyond the scope of this work, but the existence of these remedies requires to be borne in mind, as does the fact that a contravention of any requirement or prohibition imposed by a notice is an offence: see the 1974 Act, s.33(1)(g).

**1.28**   A person guilty of an offence under the 1974 Act, s.33(1)(g) is liable on conviction in summary proceedings to imprisonment for a term not exceeding 6 months, or a fine not exceeding £20,000, or both. On a conviction on indictment the maximum term of imprisonment rises to two years with an unlimited fine as an alternative, or in addition.

**Further Guidance**

**1.29**   The Health and Safety Commission have, in addition to the Approved Code of Practice, also published two guidance works. The first of these is the "Guide to managing health and safety in construction" (HSC Books 1995, ISBN 0 7176 0755 0), and is aimed at all duty-holders under the Regulations. This Guide divides projects into five stages: (1) concept and feasibility; (2) design and planning; (3) tender/ selection stage; (4) construction phase; and (5) commissioning and handover. A summary is given of each duty-holder's key tasks at each stage. Examples are given for each stage of particular problems or situations which may arise relative to the Regulations. The chart at App. 4, below (which reproduces App. 6 of the Guide), is a useful aid in determining who is responsible and who must do what, at each stage of a project.

**1.30**   The second Guide is entitled "Designing for health and safety in construction" (HSC Books 1995, ISBN 0 7176 0807 7). It deals with the duties placed on the designer by the Regulations, gives advice on practical steps designers can take in relation to the Regulations, and describes the types of construction work which will be affected and the particular hazards which may arise.

***Status of the Guides***

**1.31**   Each of the Guides is to be read "*in conjunction with the approved code of practice*". The Guides do not have the status of the Approved Code of Practice as described in paras. 1.14 to 1.20, above, and are published for guidance only. They have, however, each been approved by the Construction Industry Advisory Committee (CONIAC) and contain the following wording:

"The guidance [in the Guide] represents what is considered to be good practice by the members of CONIAC . . . Following this guidance is not compulsory and you are free to take other action. But if you follow this guidance you will normally be doing enough to comply with the law. Health and safety inspectors seek to secure compliance with the law and may refer to this guidance as illustrating good practice."

### Citation and commencement

**1.32**  **1.**  These Regulations may be cited as the Construction (Design and Management) Regulations 1994 and shall come into force on 31st March 1995.

### GENERAL NOTE

**1.33**  Subject to the transitional provisions of reg. 23, the Regulations came into effect on March 31, 1995. However the Temporary or Mobile Construction Sites Directive (92/57: [1992] O.J. L.245/6) was required to have been implemented by December 31, 1993. Although directives generally require Member States to give effect to them by implementation in domestic law, directives can, in certain circumstances, directly create legal obligations in Member States. It is, therefore, possible, although at the time of writing untested, that areas of the Temporary or Mobile Construction Sites Directive were directly applicable as domestic law of Member States notwithstanding the hiatus between the date the Directive was to have been implemented by the United Kingdom and the date the Regulations actually came into force.

**Interpretation**

**2.**—(1)   In these Regulations, unless the context otherwise requires—   **2.01**
   "agent" in relation to any client means any person who acts as agent for
      a client in connection with the carrying on by the person of a trade,
      business or other undertaking (whether for profit or not);
   "cleaning work" means the cleaning of any window or any transparent
      or translucent wall, ceiling or roof in or on a structure where such
      cleaning involves a risk of a person falling more than 2 metres;
   "client" means any person for whom a project is carried out, whether it
      is carried out by another person or is carried out in-house;
   "construction phase" means the period of time starting when construc-
      tion work in any project starts and ending when construction work
      in that project is completed;
   "construction work" means the carrying out of any building, civil
      engineering or engineering construction work and includes any of
      the following—
      (a)   the construction, alteration, conversion, fitting out, com-
            missioning, renovation, repair, upkeep, redecoration or other
            maintenance (including cleaning which involves the use of
            water or an abrasive at high pressure or the use of substances
            classified as corrosive or toxic for the purposes of regulation 7
            of the Chemicals (Hazard Information and Packaging)
            Regulations 1993**(b)**, de-commissioning, demolition or dis-
            mantling of a structure,
      (b)   the preparation for an intended structure, including site
            clearance, exploration, investigation (but not site survey) and
            excavation, and laying or installing the foundations of the
            structure,
      (c)   the assembly of prefabricated elements to form a structure or
            the disassembly of prefabricated elements which, immedi-
            ately before such disassembly, formed a structure,
      (d)   the removal of a structure or part of a structure or of any
            product or waste resulting from demolition or dismantling of
            a structure or from disassembly of prefabricated elements
            which, immediately before such disassembly formed a struc-
            ture, and
      (e)   the installation, commissioning, maintenance, repair or re-
            moval of mechanical, electrical, gas, compressed air,
            hydraulic, telecommunications, computer or similar services
            which are normally fixed within or to a structure,

---

**(b)**   S.I. 1993/1746.

but does not include the exploration for or extraction of mineral resources or activities preparatory thereto carried out at a place where such exploration or extraction is carried out;

"contractor" means any person who carries on a trade, business or other undertaking (whether for profit or not) in connection with which he—

(a)  undertakes to or does carry out or manage construction work,

(b)  arranges for any person at work under his control (including, where he is an employer, any employee of his) to carry out or manage construction work;

"design" in relation to any structure includes drawing, design details, specification and bill of quantities (including specification of articles or substances) in relation to the stucture;

"designer" means any person who carries on a trade, business or other undertaking in connection with which he—

(a)  prepares a design, or

(b)  arranges for any person under his control (including, where he is an employer, any employee of his) to prepare a design, relating to a structure or part of a structure;

"developer" shall be construed in accordance with regulation 5(1);

"domestic client" means a client for whom a project is carried out not being a project carried out in connection with the carrying on by the client of a trade, business or other undertaking (whether for profit or not);

"health and safety file" means a file, or other record in permanent form, containing the information required by virtue of regulation 14(d);

"health and safety plan" means the plan prepared by virtue of regulation 15;

"planning supervisor" means any person for the time being appointed under regulation 6(1)(a);

"principal contractor" means any person for the time being appointed under regulation 6(1)(b);

"project" means a project which includes or is intended to include construction work;

"structure" means—

(a)  any building, steel or reinforced concrete structure (not being a building), railway line or siding, tramway line, dock, harbour, inland navigation, tunnel, shaft, bridge, viaduct, waterworks, reservoir, pipe or pipe-line (whatever, in either case, it contains or is intended to contain), cable, aqueduct, sewer, sewage works, gasholder, road, airfield, sea defence works, river works, drainage works, earthworks, lagoon, dam, wall caisson, mast, tower, pylon, underground tank, earth retaining structure, or structure designed to preserve or alter any natural feature, and any other structure similar to the foregoing, or

(b) any formwork, falsework, scaffold or other structure designed or used to provide support or means of access during construction work, or

(c) any fixed plant in respect of work which is installation, commissioning, de-commissioning or dismantling and where any such work involves a risk of a person falling more than 2 metres.

(2) In determining whether any person arranges for a person (in this paragraph called "the relevant person") to prepare a design or to carry out or manage construction work regard shall be had to the following, namely—

(a) a person does arrange for the relevant person to do a thing where—

    (i) he specifies in or in connection with any arrangement with a third person that the relevant person shall do that thing (whether by nominating the relevant person as a subcontractor to the third person or otherwise), or

    (ii) being an employer, it is done by any of his employees in-house;

(b) a person does not arrange for the relevant person to do a thing where—

    (i) being a self-employed person, he does it himself or, being in partnership it is done by any of his partners; or

    (ii) being an employer, it is done by any of his employees otherwise than in-house; or

    (iii) being a firm carrying on its business anywhere in Great Britain whose principal place of business is in Scotland, it is done by any partner in the firm; or

    (iv) having arranged for a third person to do the thing, he does not object to the third person arranging for it to be done by the relevant person,

and the expressions "arrange" and "arranges" shall be construed accordingly.

(3) For the purposes of these Regulations—

(a) a project is carried out in-house where an employer arranges for the project to be carried out by an employee of his who acts, or by a group of employees who act, in either case, in relation to such a project as a separate part of the undertaking of the employer distinct from the part for which the project is carried out; and

(b) construction work is carried out or managed in-house where an employer arranges for the construction work to be carried out or managed by an employee of his who acts, or by a group of employees who act, in either case, in relation to such construction work as a separate part of the undertaking of the employer distinct from the part for which the construction work is carried out or managed; and

(c) a design is prepared in-house where an employer arranges for the design to be prepared by an employee of his who acts, or by a group of employees who act, in either case, in relation to such design as a separate part of the undertaking of the employer distinct from the part for which the design is prepared.

(4)   For the purposes of these Regulations, a project is notifiable if the construction phase—

(a)   will be longer than 30 days; or

(b)   will involve more than 500 person days of construction work,

and the expression "notifiable" shall be construed accordingly.

(5)   Any reference in these Regulations to a person being reasonably satisfied—

(a)   as to another person's competence is a reference to that person being satisfied after the taking of such steps as it is reasonable for that person to take (including making reasonable enquiries or seeking advice where necessary) to satisfy himself as to such competence; and

(b)   as to whether another person has allocated or will allocate adequate resources is a reference to that person being satisfied that after the taking of such steps as it is reasonable for that person to take (including making reasonable enquiries or seeking advice where necessary)—

(i)   to ascertain what resources have been or are intended to be so allocated; and

(ii)   to establish whether the resources so allocated or intended to be allocated are adequate.

(6)   Any reference in these References to—

(a)   a numbered regulation or Schedule is a reference to the regulation in or Schedule to these Regulations so numbered; and

(b)   a numbered paragraph is a reference to the paragraph so numbered in the regulation in which the reference appears.

## GENERAL NOTE

**2.02**   This is a general interpretation regulation. This regulation also refers (as interpreted by reg. 2(3)) to the intended meaning of: a project being carried out in-house; construction work being carried out or managed in-house; and a design being prepared in-house. This regulation further refers (as interpreted by reg. 2(5)) to the intended meaning of: a person being reasonably satisfied as to another person's competence; and a person being reasonably satisfied as to whether another person has allocated or will allocate adequate resources.

### Regulation 2(1) including Private Finance Initiative

#### Construction Work

**2.03**   The term "construction work" is new, and marks a departure from the use of the terms "building operation" and "work of engineering construction" each of which is defined in the Factories Act 1961, s.175(1). The consultative document issued by the Health and Safety Commission entitled Proposals for Construction (Design and Management) Regulations and Approved Code of Practice stated that the aim of this new term was to

"establish a comprehensive and logical framework which brings into scope the

14

full range of construction work and which removes as many as possible of the anomalies and areas of doubt associated with the existing definitions ... to include all the works covered by the [Temporary or Mobile Construction Sites Directive] ... [and] to bring into scope all the activities covered by International Labour Organisation Convention 167 on safety and health in construction."

It was also stated to be the Health and Safety Commission's intention to bring existing regulations into line with the new definition, probably in the regulations implementing the Temporary or Mobile Construction Sites Directive, Annex IV.

### *Client*

The exact scope of the term "client" is unclear from the definition. It appears that a **2.04** client could include not only an employer under a building contract, but also *e.g.* a party providing finance in connection with construction works (especially where such a party was, in certain circumstances, entitled to step into the shoes of the employer under the building contract). Where a consortium, or a joint venture company is carrying out works, the term client could be interpreted as applying to each member of the consortium or each joint venture partner, whether it plays an active part in the construction process or not. Particular problems of interpretation could arise in relation to flats where a landlord may fall within the definition of a client if it benefits from works carried out by the tenants, or where the landlord contributes financially to such works.

### *Private Finance Initiative*

Where a project is being carried out under the Private Finance Initiative (*i.e.* **2.05** whereby a major infrastructure scheme such as a hospital or sewage plant traditionally financed by the public sector is designed, constructed, financed and operated for a fixed term by the private sector) opinions appear to differ as to who is properly the "client" for the purposes of the Regulations. Under a PFI project the promoting authority (*e.g.* an NHS Trust, local authority or, in Scotland, a Water Authority) will normally pass on all design and construction risk to a consortium which in turn will enter into the design and construction contracts. The consortium will generally be granted a lease of the site of the proposed project. Thus, so the argument goes, the consortium and not the promoting authority will be the client. Given the fairly wide definition of "client" and "project" in reg. 2, this argument seems rather tenuous. Somewhat surprisingly one often finds a contract governing a PFI project containing words along the lines that "*the [authority] does not consider itself to be the client for the purposes of the CDM Regulations for the following reasons* ...". This seems rather pointless. The question of who is the client depends upon the proper interpretation of the Regulations and their application to the circumstances of the particular case. It would seem more appropriate, and consistent with the PFI principle of "risk transfer", that the consortium be appointed as agent under reg. 4 and thereby assume the obligations of the client (see paras. 4.02–4.06, below). This would, however, still leave the authority with the problem of deciding whether it has a duty to appoint a planning supervisor for the period prior to concluding the contract with the consortium and appointing it as agent under reg. 4. (See discussion on this point in paras. 6.07–6.08, below).

### *Construction Phase*

As defined the "construction phase" ends when "construction work in that project **2.06** is completed". As a project may well differ in scope from what are often termed the contract works under a building contract, the end of the construction phase may be difficult to pinpoint. The Approved Code of Practice, para. 6, provides some assistance by suggesting that the construction phase will normally end "on transfer of the structure to the client" and that "remedial work after the construction work of the project has finished should be treated as a separate project". This raises the possibility that projects carried out during a defects liability or maintenance period under a building or engineering contract should be treated as a separate project for the purposes of the Regulations.

### Demolition

**2.07**    The scope of the definition of "demolition" lacks clarity, and it is understood that the Health and Safety Executive have sought legal advice to clarify the matter. Previous suggestions as to the scope of "demolition" have included "the demolition of a load bearing part of a structure".

### Domestic Client

**2.08**    The definition of "domestic client" is also vague, particularly as applied to shared equity properties or, for example, a tenement block where some properties may be owner-occupied whilst others may be owned by, for example, investment companies or housing associations or local authorities. In such a case it is unclear whether works carried out on the block, which would otherwise be subject to the Regulations, would be a project for a domestic client. It is understood that the Health and Safety Executive have sought legal advice as to the application of the Regulations in such circumstances and that further guidance may be available shortly.

### Project

**2.09**    It is understood that the Health and Safety Executive have sought legal advice to clarify the definition of "project". Whether or not certain works constitute one project or a number of projects is clearly of great importance since, whilst the Regulations may otherwise apply to a particular project, they may not apply if that project were broken down into a number of smaller projects. At the time of writing there is no coherent answer to this problem, although it is understood that the Health and Safety Executive will be particularly concerned with high hazard, high risk projects.

### Regulation 2(4)

**2.10**    According to the Approved Code of Practice, para. 27, in determining whether or not a project is notifiable the following should be considered: "*a working day is any day on which any construction work is carried out, even if the work is of short duration or the day is a holiday or over a weekend*"; and "*A person day is one individual ... carrying out construction work for one normal working shift*". Whilst this may be of some assistance it still leaves some scope for misinterpretation or confusion.

### Regulation 2(5)    Client.

**2.11**    The requirement for the client to select only those who are competent to carry out the works is a recurring theme throughout the Regulations. Competence itself is not defined in reg. 2(5) though the Approved Code of Practice does detail the steps to be taken into account in assessing competence (see General Note to reg. 8—para. 8.02, below).

### DEFINITIONS

**2.12**    "agent": reg. 2(1).
"arrange": reg. 2(2).
"arranges": reg. 2(2).
"cleaning work": reg. 2(1).
"client": reg. 2(1).
"construction phase": reg. 2(1).

"construction work": reg. 2(1).
"contractor": reg. 2(1).
"design": reg. 2(1).
"designer": reg. 2(1).
"developer": reg. 2(1).
"domestic client": reg. 2(1).
"health and safety file": reg. 2(1).
"health and safety plan": reg. 2(1).
"notifiable": reg. 2(4).
"planning supervisor": reg. 2(1).
"principal contractor": reg. 2(1).
"project": reg. 2(1).
"structure": reg. 2(1).
"the relevant person": reg. 2(2).

## Application of regulations

**3.01**  **3.**—(1)  Subject to the following paragraphs of this regulation, these Regulations shall apply to and in relation to construction work.

(2)  Subject to paragraph (3), regulations 4 to 12 and 14 to 19 shall not apply to or in relation to construction work included in a project where the client has reasonable grounds for believing that—

(a)  the project is not notifiable; and

(b)  the largest number of persons at work at any one time carrying out construction work included in the project will be or, as the case may be, is less than 5.

(3)  These Regulations shall apply to and in relation to construction work which is the demolition or dismantling of a structure notwithstanding paragraph (2).

(4)  These Regulations shall not apply to or in relation to construction work in respect of which the local authority within the meaning of regulation 2(1) of the Health and Safety (Enforcing Authority) Regulations 1989**(a)** is the enforcing authority.

(5)  Regulation 14(b) shall not apply to projects in which no more than one designer is involved.

(6)  Regulation 16(1)(a) shall not apply to projects in which no more than one contractor is involved.

(7)  Where construction work is carried out or managed in-house or a design is prepared in-house, then, for the purposes of paragraphs (5) and (6), each part of the undertaking of the employer shall be treated as a person and shall be counted as a designer or, as the case may be, contractor, accordingly.

(8)  Except where regulation 5 applies, regulations 4, 6, 8 to 12 and 14 to 19 shall not apply to or in relation to construction work included or intended to be included in a project carried out for a domestic client.

### GENERAL NOTE

**3.02**  The Regulations apply only to construction work (see comment on the definition of "construction work" in para. 2.03, above). The regulation goes on to detail those projects where the Regulations either shall not apply or shall have limited effect. One important restriction on the extent of the applicability of the Regulations is that they impose duties only on those clients acting in connection with a trade, business or other undertaking. The undertaking need not, however, be for profit. A charity can, therefore, be a client. Under reg. 3(6) the Regulations have limited effect on domestic clients carrying out construction work on domestic premises used solely as a private dwelling. Of particular assistance in establishing whether or not the Regulations apply is the flow chart (reproduced in App. 2, below) on page 4 of the Guide to managing health and safety in construction (see para. 1.29, above).

---

(a)  S.I. 1989/1903.

18

**Regulation 3(2)**   client

If a client has reasonable grounds for believing that a project is not notifiable, and **3.03** less than 5 people are carrying out construction work at any one time, regs. 4–12 and 14–19 shall not apply. Reg. 13 (Requirements on designer) will still apply. However, where the construction work involves the demolition or dismantling of a structure, the Regulations shall apply without any restriction. The flow chart (reproduced in App. 3, below) on page 6 of the Guide to managing health and safety in construction (see para. 1.29, above) is helpful in determining whether or not a project is notifiable.

**Regulation 3(3)**

This is the only exception to the exclusion referred to in reg. 3(2).   **3.04**

**Regulation 3(4)**

The Regulations shall not apply where a local authority is the enforcing authority **3.05** for the construction work. The Health and Safety (Enforcing Authority) Regulations 1989 (S.I. 1989 No. 1903), reg. 2(1), determines whether Health and Safety Executive inspectors or local authority inspectors are responsible for enforcing health and safety legislation (the Executive has power under the said regulations to act as final arbiter). The premises for which local authorities are responsible are detailed in Sched. 1 of those Regulations and include:

1. The sale or storage of goods for retail or wholesale distribution except—
    (a) where it is part of the business of a transport undertaking;
    (b) at container depots where the main activity is the storage of goods in the course of transit to or from dock premises, an airport or a railway;
    (c) where the main activity is the sale or storage for wholesale distribution of any dangerous substance;
    (d) where the main activity is the sale or storage of water or sewage or their related by-products or natural or town gas;

   and where the main activity carried on in premises is the sale and fitting of motor car tyres, exhausts, windscreens or sunroofs the main activity shall be deemed to be the sale of goods.
2. The display or demonstration of goods at an exhibition for the purposes of offer or advertisement for sale.
3. Office activities.
4. Catering services.
5. The provision of permanent or temporary residential accommodation including the provision of a site for caravans or campers.
6. Consumer services provided in a shop except dry cleaning or radio and television repairs, and in this paragraph "consumer services" means services of a type ordinarily supplied to persons who receive them otherwise than in the course of a trade, business or other undertaking carried on by them (whether for profit or not).
7. Cleaning (wet or dry) in coin-operated units in launderettes and similar premises.
8. The use of a bath, sauna or solarium, massaging, hair transplanting, skin piercing, manicuring or other cosmetic services and therapeutic treatments, except where they are carried out under the supervisionary control of a registered medical practitioner, a dentist registered under the Dentists Act 1984 (c. 24), a physiotherapist, an osteopath or a chiropractor.
9. The practice or presentation of the arts, sports, games, entertainment or other cultural or recreational activities except where carried on in a

museum, art gallery or theatre or where the main activity is the exhibition of a cave to the public.

10. The hiring out of pleasure craft for use on inland waters.
11. The care, treatment, accommodation or exhibition of animals, birds or other creatures, except where the main activity is horse breeding or horse training at a stable, or is an agricultural activity or veterinary surgery.
12. The activities of an undertaker, except where the main activity is embalming or the making of coffins.
13. Church worship or religious meetings.

**Regulation 3(5)** *designer*

**3.06**  Where only one designer is involved in a project the planning supervisor's duty to ensure reasonable co-operation between designers (reg. 14(b)) shall not apply.

**Regulation 3(6)** *contractor*

**3.07**  Where only one contractor is involved in a project, the principal contractor's duty to ensure reasonable co-operation between all contractors (reg. 16(1)(a)) shall not apply.

**Regulation 3(7)** *client*

**3.08**  This requires that undertakings carrying out in-house construction work, to which the Regulations apply, must still carry out the duties applicable to a client when appointing their in-house staff to carry out contracting or design work. It may, therefore, be important for such undertakings to undertake internal checks to ensure that their in-house teams have the appropriate competence and resources.

**Regulation 3(8)**

**3.09**  Where the construction work is carried out for a domestic client, and no arrangement has been made with a developer as envisaged by reg. 5, then regs. 4, 6, 8–12 and 14–19 shall not apply. Accordingly only reg. 7 (Notification of project) and reg. 13 (Requirements on designer) shall apply.

**DEFINITIONS**

**3.10**  "client": reg. 2.
"contractor": reg. 2.
"construction work": reg. 2.
"design": reg. 2.
"designer": reg. 2.
"domestic client": reg. 2.
"notifiable": reg. 2.
"project": reg. 2.
"structure": reg. 2.

## Clients and agents of clients

**4.**—(1)   A client may appoint an agent or another client to act as the only **4.01** client in respect of a project and where such an appointment is made the provisions of paragraphs (2) to (5) shall apply.

(2)   No client shall appoint any person as his agent under paragraph (1) unless the client is reasonably satisfied that the person he intends to appoint as his agent has the competence to perform the duties imposed on a client by these Regulations.

(3)   Where the person appointed under paragraph (1) makes a declaration in accordance with paragraph (4), then from the date of receipt of the declaration by the Executive, such requirements and prohibitions as are imposed by these Regulations upon a client shall apply to the person so appointed (so long as he remains as such) as if he were the only client in respect of that project.

(4)   A declaration in accordance with this paragraph—

(a)   is a declaration in writing, signed by or on behalf of the person referred to in paragraph (3), to the effect that the client or agent who makes it will act as client for the purposes of these Regulations; and

(b)   shall include the name of the person by or on behalf of whom it is made, the address where documents may be served on that person and the address of the construction site; and

(c)   shall be sent to the Executive.

(5)   Where the Executive receives a declaration in accordance with paragraph (4), it shall give notice to the person by or on behalf of whom the declaration is made and the notice shall include the date the declaration was received by the Executive.

(6)   Where the person referred to in paragraph (3) does not make a declaration in accordance with paragraph (4), any requirement or prohibition imposed by these Regulations on a client shall also be imposed on him but only to the extent it relates to any matter within his authority.

## GENERAL NOTE

This regulation allows a client, upon sending a declaration in the prescribed form **4.02** to the Executive, to appoint an agent or another client to undertake the obligations imposed under regs. 6 and 8–12. This may be of assistance in cases where there is more than one client or where it is deemed appropriate to transfer or allocate the risk associated with being a client under the Regulations to another party. See, *e.g.* comments in para. 2.05, above, in relation to PFI projects. Where a declaration is made the duties of a client imposed by the Regulations apply to the person so appointed (as long as he remains appointed) as if he were the only client. In other words, a person who would otherwise be a client may transfer his duties by means of a declaration under reg. 4. However, where no declaration is made following an appointment, both the "original" client and the appointee (to the extent that the duties relate to any matter within his authority) will be responsible for the carrying out of the client duties imposed by the Regulations. Reg. 4(3) requires the appointee to make the declaration. It is clearly in the "original" client's interest to ensure that this is done and that the Executive's acknowledgment under reg. 4(5) is received.

**4.03**   This regulation shall not apply, by virtue of reg. 3(2), to construction work in a project if the client has reasonable grounds for believing that the project is not notifiable and the number of people carrying out construction work at any one time is less than 5.

**4.04**   This regulation shall also not apply, by virtue of reg. 3(8), where construction work in a project is carried out for a domestic client unless the client has made an arrangement with a developer under reg. 5.

**Regulation 4(2)**   Client.

**4.05**   In appointing an agent or another client under reg. 4(1), the client should be reasonably satisfied as to the competence of the appointee in performing the duties placed on a client under the Regulations. The Regulations do not explicitly state what is required in order for a client to be reasonably satisfied as to competence in this context (although some guidance is given in the Approved Code of Practice at paras. 17 and 18), but this must relate to the competence of the appointee to perform the client's duties under the Regulations. The level of inquiries required will inevitably vary according to the particular project in question and its size and complexity. See also the annotations in respect of regs. 8 and 9 (paras. 8.02–8.07 and 9.02–9.04, below, respectively).

**DEFINITIONS**

**4.06**   "agent": reg. 2.
"client": reg. 2.
"Executive": Health and Safety at Work etc. Act 1974, s.53(1).
"project": reg. 2.

**Requirements on developer**

**5.**—(1)   This regulation applies where the project is carried out for a   **5.01**
domestic client and the client enters into an arrangement with a person (in
this regulation called "the developer") who carries on a trade, business or
other undertaking (whether for profit or not) in connection with which—
  (a)   land or an interest in land is granted or transferred to the client; and
  (b)   the developer undertakes that construction work will be carried out
         on the land; and
  (c)   following the construction work, the land will include premises
         which, as intended by the client, will be occupied as a residence.
  (2)   Where this regulation applies, with effect from the time the client
enters into the arrangement referred to in paragraph (1), the requirements
of regulations 6 and 8 to 12 shall apply to the developer as if he were the
client.

**GENERAL NOTE**

This regulation is intended to apply to those instances where a developer agrees to   **5.02**
procure the land for, and subsequent construction of, domestic premises, or sell such
premises before completion of construction work to a domestic client. In such
instances reg. 6 (Appointments of planning supervisor and principal contractor), reg.
8 (Competence of planning supervisor, designers and contractors), reg. 9 (Provision
for health and safety), reg. 10 (Start of construction phase), reg. 11 (Client to ensure
information is available) and reg. 12 (Client to ensure health and safety file is
available for inspection) shall apply to the developer as if he were the client.

**Derogation**

This regulation shall not apply, by virtue of reg. 3(2), to construction work in a   **5.03**
project if the client has reasonable grounds for believing that the project is not
notifiable and the number of people carrying out construction work at one time is less
than 5.

**DEFINITIONS**

"client": reg. 2.   **5.04**
"construction work": reg. 2.
"domestic client": reg. 2.
"project": reg. 2.
"the developer": reg. 5(1).

### Appointments of planning supervisor and principal contractor

**6.01**   **6.**—(1)   Subject to paragraph (6)(b), every client shall appoint—

(a)   a planning supervisor; and

(b)   a principal contractor,

in respect of each project.

(2)   The client shall not appoint as principal contractor any person who is not a contractor.

(3)   The planning supervisor shall be appointed as soon as is practicable after the client has such information about the project and the construction work involved in it as will enable the client to comply with the requirements imposed on him by regulations 8(1) and 9(1).

(4)   The principal contractor shall be appointed as soon as is practicable after the client has such information about the project and the construction work involved in it as will enable the client to comply with the requirements imposed on him by regulations 8(3) and 9(3) when making such an arrangement with a contractor to manage construction work where such arrangement consists of the appointment of the principal contractor.

(5)   The appointments mentioned in paragraph (1) shall be terminated, changed or renewed as necessary to ensure that those appointments remain filled at all times until the end of the construction phase.

(6)   Paragraph (1) does not prevent—

(a)   the appointment of the same person as planning supervisor and as principal contractor provided that person is competent to carry out the functions under these Regulations of both appointments; or

(b)   the appointment of the client as planning supervisor or as principal contractor or as both, provided the client is competent to perform the relevant functions under these Regulations.

**GENERAL NOTE**

---

**6.02**     The client is required to appoint a planning supervisor and principal contractor for each project. The timing of these appointments is fundamental to the Regulations' aims of putting health and safety planning to the forefront of the minds of the client, designers and contractors at the start of any project. The imposition of this duty on the client is therefore a significant reallocation of the risk involved in any project. There is no restriction on who may fulfil the role of planning supervisor or principal contractor, save that the principal contractor must be a contractor. Either role may be fulfilled by any legal entity, whether an individual, partnership, private or public limited company. Reg. 6(6) makes the scope of appointment wider by allowing the same person to be both planning supervisor and principal contractor. The latitude allowed by reg. 6(6) is of particular assistance to those forms of procurement, such as design and build, where one entity will undertake a number of roles and/or where single point responsibility is desired (but see para. 6.07, below). While reg. 6(5) requires the planning supervisor and principal contractor roles to remain in existence until the end of the construction phase, it provides some flexibility by allowing the appointments to be changed during the course of the project. Thus the roles may be carried out by, *e.g.* one party during the outline planning stages of a project and by another during the work on site. However, throughout the construction phase, it remains the client's duty to ensure that whoever is appointed as planning supervisor and/or principal contractor is competent to perform that role.

### Transitional Provisions

The transitional provisions referred to in reg. 23, and detailed in Sched. 2 to the Regulations apply to this regulation, with the effect that this regulation shall not apply if the construction phase of a project started before March 31, 1995. **6.03**

### Derogation

This regulation shall not apply, by virtue of reg. 3(2), to construction work in a project if the client has reasonable grounds for believing that the project is not notifiable and the number of people carrying out construction work is less than 5. **6.04**

This regulation also shall not apply, by virtue of reg. 3(8), where construction work in a project is carried out for a domestic client unless the client has made an arrangement with a developer under reg. 5. **6.05**

### Practicable and Reasonably Practicable

It is interesting to note that a distinction is drawn in the Regulations between those duties required to be carried out as soon as is "practicable", as in regs. 6 and 7, and those which are required to be carried out as soon as is "reasonably practicable", as in regs. 10, 11, 13–17 and 19—see General Note to reg. 10 (para. 10.05, below). **6.06**

### Design and build contracts

It may often appear appropriate in a design and build contract for the design and build contractor to be appointed planning supervisor (and it will almost invariably be the principal contractor too). Advantages can therefore be taken of reg. 6(6)(a)—see para. 6.02, above. However, particularly where the contract is procured by competitive tender, there is likely to be a significant time lapse between the initial concept and feasibility stage and the preparation of tender documents. Under the above scenario the planning supervisor clearly cannot be appointed until the design and build contract is in place. In those circumstances who is responsible for carrying out the planning supervisor's tasks during the pre-tender stage, such as the preparation of the pre-tender health and safety plan to be included in the tender documents? The not wholly satisfactory solution proposed by the Approved Code of Practice, para. 21, is that "*it may be appropriate to appoint a planning supervisor to oversee the initial concept and definition of the project, and to confirm the appointment, or make a new one as required by regulation 6(5), when the design and build contractor has been appointed*". This presumes that the client will undertake the "initial concept" of the project, which may not always be a valid presumption—see para. 6.08, below. **6.07**

### Health and Safety Plan

The point at which the planning supervisor is to be appointed is not entirely clear. The terms of reg. 6(3) are somewhat circular. In practice the timing of the appointment will be governed by the need to produce a pre-tender health and safety plan before arrangements for carrying out or managing the construction works are **6.08** completed (reg. 15(2)). According to the Approved Code of Practice, para. 77, the health and safety plan needs to be sufficiently developed for it to form part of the tender documentation. However there may be situations (*e.g.* in a PFI project as described in para. 2.05, above) where no meaningful design, even of a conceptual nature, is carried out during the pre-contract phase, and all design is, therefore, carried out by or on behalf of the contractor. In the absence of any significant design it is arguably not possible to identify hazards and risks arising from the existing environment and the proposed design and/or construction materials to allow a worthwhile health and safety plan to be prepared. Does a planning supervisor still require to be appointed (and a health and safety plan prepared—for what it is worth)? Does a client under a PFI project require to appoint a planning supervisor for the pre-contact period notwithstanding that it intends to appoint the successful consortium as its agent under reg. 4 (see also para. 2.05, above)? Unfortunately neither the Regulations nor the Approved Code of Practice provide an answer to these questions. This illustrates the tendency of both the Regulations and the Approved Code of Practice to take into account only the conventional and traditional methods of construction contract procurement, and to leave the position somewhat vague in relation to the more unorthodox or novel.

## DEFINITIONS

**6.09**    "client": reg. 2.
"construction phase": reg. 2.
"construction work": reg. 2.
"contractor": reg. 2.
"planning supervisor": reg. 2.
"principal contractor": reg. 2.
"project": reg. 2.

**Notification of project**

**7.**—(1)   The planning supervisor shall ensure that notice of the project in **7.01** respect of which he is appointed is given to the Executive in accordance with paragraphs (2) to (4) unless the planning supervisor has reasonable grounds for believing that the project is not notifiable.

(2)   Any notice required by paragraph (1) shall be given in writing or in such other manner as the Executive may from time to time approve in writing and shall contain the particulars specified in paragraph (3) or, where applicable, paragraph (4) and shall be given at the times specified in those paragraphs.

(3)   Notice containing such of the particulars specified in Schedule 1 as are known or can reasonably be ascertained shall be given as soon as is practicable after the appointment of the planning supervisor.

(4)   Where any particulars specified in Schedule 1 have not been notified under paragraph (3), notice of such particulars shall be given as soon as is practicable after the appointment of the principal contractor and, in any event, before the start of construction work.

(5)   Where a project is carried out for a domestic client then, except where regulation 5 applies, every contractor shall ensure that notice of the project is given to the Executive in accordance with paragraph (6) unless the contractor has reasonable grounds for believing that the project is not notifiable.

(6)   Any notice required by paragraph (5) shall—

(a)   be in writing or such other manner as the Executive may from time to time approve in writing;

(b)   contain such of the particulars specified in Schedule 1 as are relevant to the project; and

(c)   be given before the contractor or any person at work under his control starts to carry out construction work.

**GENERAL NOTE**

A written notice, containing the details set out in the Regulations, Sched. 1, is to be **7.02** given to the Executive by the planning supervisor, in respect of notifiable projects, as soon as is practicable after the appointment of the planning supervisor (see HSE form in App. 5, below). The Approved Code of Practice, para. 27, advises that where there is doubt as to the length of the construction work, a notification should be submitted. Whilst the regulation does not expressly state to whom the notice is to be given, the Approved Code of Practice advises, at para. 29, that it should be sent to *"the HSE area office covering the site where construction work is to take place"*.

**Derogation**

**7.03**  This regulation shall not apply, by virtue of reg. 3(2), to construction work in a project if the client has reasonable grounds for believing that the project is not notifiable and the number of people carrying out construction work is less than 5.

**Practicable and Reasonably Practicable**

**7.04**  See the comments on distinction between "practicable" and "reasonably practicable" in General Note to annotations for regs. 6 and 10 (para. 6.06, above and para. 10.05, below, respectively).

**Regulation 7(5)**  *contractor*

**7.05**  Where notifiable work is carried out for a domestic client and there is no developer, as envisaged by reg. 5, then each contractor engaged on the project is under a duty to submit notification of the project to the Executive. There is no reason why a lead contractor should not submit notification on behalf of all contractors engaged in the project, provided the notification makes clear that this is what is being done.

**DEFINITIONS**

**7.06**  "contractor": reg. 2.
"construction work": reg. 2.
"domestic client": reg. 2.
"Executive": Health and Safety at Work etc. Act 1974, s.53(1).
"notifiable": reg. 2.
"planning supervisor": reg. 2.
"principal contractor": reg. 2.
"project": reg. 2.

### Competence of planning supervisor, designers and contractors

**8.**—(1)   No client shall appoint any person as planning supervisor in respect of a project unless the client is reasonably satisfied that the person he intends to appoint has the competence to perform the functions of planning supervisor under these Regulations in respect of that project.  **8.01**

(2)   No person shall arrange for a designer to prepare a design unless he is reasonably satisfied that the designer has the competence to prepare that design.

(3)   No person shall arrange for a contractor to carry out or manage construction work unless he is reasonably satisfied that the contractor has the competence to carry out or, as the case may be, manage, that construction work.

(4)   Any reference in this regulation to a person having competence shall extend only to his competence—

(a)   to perform any requirement; and

(b)   to conduct his undertaking without contravening any prohibition, imposed on him by or under any of the relevant statutory provisions.

### GENERAL NOTE

In appointing the planning supervisor, a client or, under reg. 4, its agent, must be reasonably satisfied as to the planning supervisor's competence to comply with its duties under the Regulations. Competence in this context refers to the ability to comply with the Regulations, and not to technical competence. It is not of course necessarily the client who will appoint designers and contractors and in such cases the obligation to make inquiries falls onto the relevant duty-holder making the appointment. In many construction projects this would mean a sub-contractor or sub-consultant. Reg. 8(4) provides that in assessing competence the client, or relevant duty-holder, need make only reasonable inquiries, which suggests that inquiries must be tailored to the circumstances of particular projects, including the size and complexity of the project. In assessing responses to inquiries the client or duty-holder may require to seek specialist advice in relation to certain aspects of the project. Competence should also be assessed in relation to any particular procurement method involved on the project and also the terms of appointment of the relevant appointee. The Approved Code of Practice states (para. 35) that those making the checks need to take into account the need for (1) a knowledge and understanding of the work involved, the management and prevention of risk and of relevant health and safety standards; and (2) the capacity to apply this knowledge and experience to the work required in relation to the particular project for which the planning supervisor, designer or contractor is being engaged.  **8.02**

#### Derogation

This regulation shall not apply, by virtue of reg. 3(2), to construction work in a project if the client has reasonable grounds for believing that the project is not notifiable and the number of people carrying out construction work is less than 5.  **8.03**

**8.04**     This regulation shall also not apply, by virtue of reg. 3(8), where construction work in a project is carried out for a domestic client unless the client has made an arrangement under reg. 5.

### Regulation 8(1)

**8.05**     The Approved Code of Practice suggests, at para. 38, that reasonable steps to take, in assessing the competence of a planning supervisor to carry out its duties under regs. 14 and 15(1), may include checking: (1) membership of a relevant professional body; (2) the planning supervisor's knowledge of construction practice, particularly in relation to the nature of the project; (3) familiarity and knowledge of the design function; (4) knowledge of health and safety issues (including fire safety issues), particularly in preparing a health and safety plan; (5) ability to work with and co-ordinate the activities of different designers and be a bridge between the design function and construction work on the site; (6) the number, experience and qualifications of people to be employed, both internally and from other sources, to perform the various functions in relation to the project; (7) the management systems which will be used to monitor the correct allocation of people and other resources; (8) the time to be allowed to carry out the different duties; and (9) the technical facilities available to aid the staff in carrying out their duties.

### Regulation 8(2) Designer·

**8.06**     Para. 40 of the Approved Code of Practice suggests that reasonable steps to take, in assessing the competence of a designer to carry out its duties under reg. 13, may include checking: (1) membership of a relevant professional organisation; (2) familiarity with construction processes in the circumstances of the project and the impact of design on health and safety; (3) awareness of relevant health and safety and fire safety legislation and appropriate risk assessment methods; (4) the health and safety practices of the designer for design work carried out; (5) the people to be employed to carry out the work, their skills and training; this will include external resources where necessary, and review of the design against the requirements of reg. 13; (6) the time allowed to fulfil the designer's works; (7) the technical facilities available to support the designer, particularly in the circumstances of the project; (8) the method of communicating design decisions to ensure that the resources to be allocated are clear; and (9) the way in which information on the remaining risks, after the duties in reg. 13(2)(a) have been complied with, will be communicated.

### Regulation 8(3) Contractor·

**8.07**     According to para. 46 of the Approved Code of Practice, the reasonable steps to take, in assessing the competence of a principal contractor or contractor to carry out its duties under regs. 16–18 and 19 respectively, may include checking: (1) the arrangements in place to manage health and safety including fire safety; (2) the procedures adopted for developing and implementing the health and safety plan; (3) the approach to be taken to deal with high-risk areas identified by the designers and planning supervisor; (4) the arrangements for monitoring compliance with health and safety legislation; (5) the people to carry out or manage the work, their skills and training; (6) the time allowed to complete the various stages of the construction work without risks to health and safety; and (7) the way people are to be employed to ensure compliance with health and safety law. Health and safety has for some time been considered of some importance in the tendering procedure as illustrated by the 1987 Construction Industry Advisory Committee guidelines. However, there was little firm legal backing for such a factor to be taken into account at tender stage, and it is difficult to assess what practical notice of such measures was taken. Although now superseded by these Regulations, it is interesting to note that in *General*

*Building & Maintenance v. Greenwich London Borough Council, The Times*, March 9, 1993, it was held that the Council was correct not to invite General Building to tender because it had failed to meet the Council's health and safety requirements (which were based on the Public Works Contracts Regulations 1991 (S.I. 1991 No. 2680), reg. 12); health and safety being a matter which could be considered as being within the scope of the said Regulations' criteria of "technical capacity".

**DEFINITIONS**

"client": reg. 2.                                                        **8.08**
"construction work": reg. 2.
"contractor": reg. 2.
"design": reg. 2.
"designer": reg. 2.
"planning supervisor": reg. 2.
"project": reg. 2.

### Provision for health and safety

**9.01**    **9.**—(1)    No client shall appoint any person as planning supervisor in respect of a project unless the client is reasonably satisfied that the person he intends to appoint has allocated or, as appropriate, will allocate adequate resources to enable him to perform the functions of planning supervisor under these Regulations in respect of that project.

(2)    No person shall arrange for a designer to prepare a design unless he is reasonably satisfied that the designer has allocated or, as appropriate, will allocate adequate resources to enable the contractor to comply with the requirements and prohibitions imposed on him by or under the relevant statutory regulations.

### GENERAL NOTE

**9.02**    A client or its agent must in appointing the planning supervisor be reasonably satisfied that the planning supervisor will allocate adequate resources to comply with its duties under the Regulations in relation to the project. The obligation to make reasonable inquiries extends to the relevant duty-holder (which may not necessarily be the client or agent) making the appointments. See also annotations to reg. 8 (paras. 8.02–8.07, above.

#### Derogation

**9.03**    This regulation shall not apply, by virtue of reg. 3(2), to construction work in a project if the client has reasonable grounds for believing that the project is not notifiable and the number of people carrying out construction work is less than 5.

**9.04**    This regulation shall also not apply, by virtue of reg. 3(8), where construction work in a project is carried out for a domestic client unless the client has made an arrangement with a developer under reg. 5.

### DEFINITIONS

**9.05**    "client": reg. 2.
"construction work": reg. 2.
"contractor": reg. 2.
"design": reg. 2.
"designer": reg. 2.
"planning supervisor": reg. 2.
"project": reg. 2.

**Start of construction phase**

**10.** Every client shall ensure, so far as is reasonably practicable, ~~that the~~ **10.01** construction phase of any project does not start unless a health and safety plan complying with regulation 15(4) has been prepared in respect of that project.

## GENERAL NOTE

While the planning supervisor has the duty to prepare the health and safety plan, **10.02** the client is responsible for ensuring, so far as is reasonably practicable, that the construction phase does not start unless an appropriate health and safety plan has been prepared. In practice the client will normally rely on professional advice, particularly that of the planning supervisor, who has a duty under reg. 14(c)(ii) to give adequate advice to allow the client to comply with this regulation. This effect of this regulation is that the health and safety plan, originally developed by the planning supervisor and then transferred to the principal contractor, must be completed before the work begins on site. See also comment on distinction between "practicable" and "reasonably practicable" in para. 6.06, above, and para. 10.05, below. The use of "reasonably practicable" in reg. 10 may accommodate certain fast-track procurement methods where work is developed in packages and the design of some packages will only be completed after the work has already begun on site. In that case the clients duty can, prior to commencement of the construction phase, only extend to those packages where the design has been sufficiently prepared. There would, therefore, be a rolling programme of developing the health and safety plan as each package became complete and ready to commence the construction phase.

The Approved Code of Practice, para. 49, states that once the construction phase **10.03** has commenced, neither the client nor the planning supervisor is under a duty to check that the plan complies with reg. 15. However, it is misleading to suggest that either party's involvement with the health and safety plan ends once the construction phase begins. If, for whatever reason, a change and/or variation becomes necessary in a project, and that change and/or variation could affect the design and/or management of the construction work, then it is arguable that the planning supervisor has a continuing duty under reg. 14(e) to ensure that the principal contractor does amend the health and safety plan to accommodate the change and/or variation. The approach is confirmed by references in the Approved Code of Practice to the need to make provision for such changes in the health and safety plan (Approved Code of Practice, App. 4), and also for the planning supervisor and principal contractor to agree on changes, in order for the planning supervisor to comply with its duty under reg. 14 (Approved Code of Practice, para. 87).

By virtue of reg. 21 (see paras. 21.02–21.10, below) an action for breach of the **10.04** statutory duty contained within this regulation may be pursued. The only other provision of the Regulations in respect of which such an action may be pursued is reg. 16(1)(c) (see para. 16.08, below).

**Practicable and Reasonably Practicable**

The regulation imposes a standard of reasonable practicability (see para. 6.06, **10.05** above). Neither the Regulations nor the Health and Safety at Work etc. Act 1974 define the expression "so far as is practicable", nor the expression "so far as is reasonably practicable". The Oxford English Dictionary definition of "practicable", *i.e.* that which is capable of being carried out in action or that which is feasible, was applied by the Court of Appeal in the case of *Lee v. Nursery Furnishings Ltd* [1945] 1 All E.R. 387. Prefixing "practicable" with "reasonably" creates a qualification whereby the extent of any risk requires to be balanced against the measures necessary to avert that risk, a form of cost benefit analysis. See *Sharp v. Coltness Iron Co. Ltd* 1937 S.C. (H.L.) 68, in particular the speech of Lord MacMillan at 78 and *Edwards v. N.C.B.* [1949] 1 K.B. 704, subsequently approved by the House of Lords in *Marshall v. Gotham Co. Ltd* [1954] A.C. 360. What is reasonably practicable depends on whether the time, trouble and expense of the precautions suggested are disproportionate to the risk involved, see the speech of Lord Oaksey in *Marshall*. It is in short a balancing act. What is reasonable for a large undertaking may be unreasonable for a small undertaking. It should be noted that "reasonably practicable" has been held to have a narrower meaning than "physically possible": see the decision of the Court of Appeal in *Marshall v. Gotham Co. Ltd* [1953] 1 Q.B. 167 and in particular the judgment of Jenkins L.J. It must be borne in mind that the breach of statutory duty must cause or materially contribute to the injury sustained. It is difficult to see how a breach of reg. 10 alone could cause injury.

**Derogation**

**10.06**  This regulation shall not apply, by virtue of reg. 3(2), to construction work in a project if the client has reasonable grounds for believing that the project is not notifiable and the number of people carrying out construction work is less than 5.

**10.07**  This regulation also shall not apply, by virtue of reg. 3(8), where construction work in a project is carried out for a domestic client unless the client has made an arrangement with a developer under reg. 5.

**DEFINITIONS**

**10.08**  "client": reg. 2.
"construction phase": reg. 2.
"health and safety plan": reg. 2.
"project": reg. 2.

**Client to ensure information is available**

**11.**—(1)   Every client shall ensure that the planning supervisor for any   **11.01**
project carried out for the client is provided (as soon as is reasonably
practicable but in any event before the commencement of the work to which
the information relates) with all information mentioned in paragraph (2)
about the state or condition of any premises at or on which construction
work included or intended to be included in the project is or is intended to be
carried out.

(2)   The information required to be provided by paragraph (1) is
information which is relevant to the functions of the planning supervisor
under these Regulations and which the client has or could ascertain by
making enquiries which it is reasonable for a person in his position to make.

## GENERAL NOTE

The purpose of this regulation is to ensure that the planning supervisor is provided   **11.02**
with sufficient information in order to comply with its duties under regs. 14 and 15(1).
The client should supply not only that information which is readily to hand, but also
such information as is obtainable by making reasonable inquiries. This could
encompass, *e.g.* making inquiries as to the previous use of land or buildings.

The suggested contents of a health and safety plan appear in App. 4 to the   **11.03**
Approved Code of Practice. These include "*existing environment*" such as ground
conditions "*e.g. contamination, gross instability, possible subsidence, old mine
workings, underground obstructions etc*". If the planning supervisor is required,
pursuant to reg. 15, to include such details in the health and safety plan, this raises the
question of the extent to which the client is obliged, by virtue of his duties under reg.
11, to provide him with the information to do so. Any statutory obligation on the
client to provide information on ground conditions may be at odds with his
contractual obligations in cases where the contractor is obliged to take the risk of
such conditions. Be that as it may, it must be said that the drafting of reg. 11, which is
one of the most important provisions as regards client duties, is not entirely
satisfactory and the scope of the client's duties under this regulation is less than clear.

**Derogation**

This regulation shall not apply, by virtue of reg. 3(2), to construction work in a   **11.04**
project if the client has reasonable grounds for believing that the project is not
notifiable and the number of people carrying out construction work is less than 5.

**Practicable and Reasonably Practicable**

See the comments on distinction between "practicable" and "reasonably practi-   **11.05**
cable" in paras. 6.06, 10.05, above.

**Health and Safety File**

The Approved Code of Practice, para. 50, provides that the information to be   **11.06**
provided will include that which is contained in any health and safety file relating to

the structure. Reg. 11 must, therefore, be read in conjunction with reg. 12. While reg. 12 obliges a client to keep the health and safety file available for inspection and deliver it to any person acquiring his interest in the property of the structure, it does not specifically require the person acquiring that interest to make sure it is delivered to him. However, in the event that the person acquiring the interest subsequently carries out to the structure works to which the Regulations apply, that person becomes the "client" for the purposes of those works and will require under reg. 11 to provide any existing health and safety file to the planning supervisor. It is, therefore, important that a new owner or tenant obtain delivery of any existing health and safety file at the time he acquires his interest in the property.

## DEFINITIONS

**11.07**    "client": reg. 2.
"construction work": reg. 2.
"planning supervisor": reg. 2.
"project": reg. 2.

**Client to ensure health and safety file is available for inspection**

**12.**—(1)   Every client shall take such steps as it is reasonable for a person **12.01**
in his position to take to ensure that the information in any health and safety
file which has been delivered to him is kept available for inspection by any
person who may need information in the file for the purpose of complying
with the requirements and prohibitions imposed on him by or under the
relevant statutory provisions.

(2)   It shall be sufficient compliance with paragraph (1) by a client who
disposes of his entire interest in the property of the structure if he delivers
the health and safety file for the structure to the person who acquires his
interest in the property of the structure and ensures such person is aware of
the nature and purpose of the health and safety file.

**GENERAL NOTE**

This regulation provides a link between a project and subsequent work carried out **12.02**
on any structure within the original project. Thus a subsequent planning supervisor
may use the health and safety file when compiling the new health and safety plan, and
can ensure that designers are given information relevant to the new project. The duty
is on the planning supervisor to procure the preparation of the health and safety file
(reg. 14(d)). However, the principal contractor is also under a duty (reg. 16(e)(ii)) to
provide information to the planning supervisor to enable the planning suprvisor to
comply with reg. 14. If reg. 12(2) is construed strictly it is only necessary for a client to
deliver the health and safety file to someone acquiring "his interest" in the property
of the structure. This suggests a like-for-like transfer, *i.e.* leaseholder (in Scotland,
tenant) to leaseholder/tenant, freehold owner (in Scotland, heritable proprietor) to
freehold owner/heritable proprietor. However, in cases where a client leases out the
whole or part of a structure then, depending upon the lease requirements, the health
and safety plan may either be transferred to the leaseholder/tenant or retained by the
client with each leaseholder/tenant being made aware of the health and safety file and
of its availability. Where health and safety files are transferred to leaseholders/
tenants it becomes important to ensure that proper updating occurs if further works
are carried out.

A potential flaw in the operation of the health and safety file provisions is that the **12.03**
obligation to pass on the health and safety file will cease if the person acquiring the
file does not instruct any construction work and therefore at no time becomes a
"client". In practice one would expect that purchasers or leaseholders (in Scotland,
tenants) will insist on any health and safety file being passed to them. As discussed at
para. 11.06, above, the existing file will be required to enable the new owner or
leaseholders/tenant to comply with reg. 11 in the event that he carries out further
work to which the Regulations apply.

**Derogation**

This regulation shall not apply, by virtue of reg. 3(2), to construction work in a **12.04**
project if the client has reasonable grounds for believing that the project is not
notifiable and the number of people carrying out construction work is less than 5.

**12.05**     This regulation shall also not apply, by virtue of reg. 3(8), where construction work in a project is carried out for a domestic client unless the client has made an arrangement with a developer under reg. 5.

## DEFINITIONS

**12.06**     "client": reg. 2.
"health and safety file": reg. 2.
"structure": reg. 2.

**Requirements on designer**

**13.**—(1)  Except where a design is prepared in-house, no employer shall  **13.01**
cause or permit any employee of his to prepare, and no self-employed
person shall prepare, a design in respect of any project unless he has taken
reasonable steps to ensure that the client for that project is aware of the
duties to which the client is subject by virtue of these Regulations and of any
practical guidance issued from time to time by the Commission with respect
to the requirements of these Regulations.

(2)  Every designer shall—

(a)  ensure that any design he prepares and which he is aware will be used
for the purposes of construction work includes among the design
consideration adequate regard to the need—

(i)  to avoid foreseeable risks to the health and safety of any
person at work carrying out construction work or cleaning
work in or on the structure at any time, or of any person who
may be affected by the work of such a person at work,

(ii)  to combat at source risks to the health and safety of any person
at work carrying out construction work or cleaning work in or
on the structure at any time or of any person who may be
affected by the work of such a person at work, and

(iii)  to give priority to measures which will protect all persons at
work who may carry out construction work or cleaning work at
any time and all persons who may be affected by the work of
such persons at work over measures which only protect each
person carrying out such work;

(b)  ensure that the design includes adequate information about any
aspect of the project or structure or materials (including articles or
substances) which might affect the health or safety of any person at
work carrying out construction work or cleaning work in or on the
structure at any time or of any person who may be affected by the
work of such a person at work; and

(c)  co-operate with the planning supervisor and with any other designer
who is preparing any design in connection with the same project or
structure so far as is necessary to enable each of them to comply with
the requirements and prohibitions placed on him in relation to the
project by or under the relevant statutory provisions.

(3)  Sub-paragraphs (a) and (b) of paragraph (2) shall require the design
to include only the matters referred to therein to the extent that it is
reasonable to expect the designer to address them at the time the design is
prepared and to the extent that it is otherwise reasonably practicable to do
so.

**GENERAL NOTE**

**13.02**     This regulation sets out the duties of the designer under the Regulations. In general the designer is under a duty to take reasonable steps to ensure that the client is aware of its duties under the Regulations, except where the design is prepared in-house. The designer appears to have a more pro-active role than the planning supervisor, since while the former must make the client aware of its duties, the latter is required (under reg. 14) only to "be in a position to give adequate advice". This is consistent with the planning supervisor's overall supervisory and co-ordinating function. The duties under reg. 13(2) are, however, not dependent upon the design of a designer being prepared for a client. It is in effect an independent obligation incumbent upon designers whenever the Regulations apply and a design is prepared by a designer for use in or in connection with construction work.

**13.03**     As the Approved Code of Practice, para. 68, states, the duties under this regulation do not

> "require architects, engineers and similar professional advisers (where they act as designers or are appointed as planning supervisor) to dictate construction methods or to exercise a health and safety management function over contractors as they carry out construction work."

However it may be difficult in some circumstances to draw the distinction between the designers obligations under reg. 13 and the extent to which these may impact upon the type of construction method to be used.

**Regulation 13(2)**    designer.

### Practicable and Reasonably Practicable

**13.04**     The distinction has already been drawn between that which is "practicable" and that which is "reasonably practicable" (see paras. 6.06 and 10.05, above). Reg. 13(3) qualifies the duties in reg. 13(2) to the extent that the designer must do that which it is reasonable for a designer to do when the design is prepared and only to the extent that it is otherwise reasonably practicable. The Approved Code of Practice, para. 56, advises that in determining what is reasonably practicable, the risk to health and safety produced by a feature of the design has to be weighed against the cost of excluding that feature by: (1) designing to avoid risks to health and safety; (2) tackling the causes of risks at source; or, if this is not possible, (3) reducing and controlling the effects of risks by means aimed at protecting anyone who might be affected by the risks and so yielding the greatest benefit. Cost should therefore be considered not simply in its financial sense but in a wider context including, as the Approved Code of Practice, para. 57, states, fitness for purpose, aesthetics, buildability or environmental impact.

**DEFINITIONS**

**13.05**     "cleaning work": reg. 2.
"client": reg. 2.
"Commission": Health and Safety at Work etc. Act 1974, s.53(1).
"construction work": reg. 2.
"design": reg. 2.
"designer": reg. 2.
"in-house": reg. 2.
"project": reg. 2.
"structure": reg. 2.

## Requirements on planning supervisor

**14.** The planning supervisor appointed for any project shall—  **14.01**
(a)  ensure, so far as is reasonably practicable, that the design of any structure comprised in the project—
    (i)  includes among the design considerations adequate regard to the needs specified in heads (i) to (iii) of regulation 13(2)(a), and
    (ii)  includes adequate information as specified in regulation 13(2)(b);
(b)  take such steps as it is reasonable for a person in his position to take to ensure co-operation between designers so far as is necessary to enable each designer to comply with the requirements placed on him by regulation 13;
(c)  be in a position to give adequate advice to—
    (i)  any client and any contractor with a view to enabling each of them to comply with regulations 8(2) and 9(2), and to
    (ii)  any client with a view to enabling him to comply with regulations 8(3), 9(3) and 10;
(d)  ensure that a health and safety file is prepared in respect of each structure comprised in the project containing—
    (i)  information included with the design by virtue of regulation 13(2)(b), and
    (ii)  any other information relating to the project which it is reasonably foreseeable will be necessary to ensure the health and safety of any person at work who is carrying out or will carry out construction work or cleaning work in or on the structure or of any person who may be affected by the work of such a person at work;
(e)  review, amend or add to the health and safety file prepared by virtue of sub-paragraph (d) of this regulation as necessary to ensure that it contains the information mentioned in that sub-paragraph when it is delivered to the client in accordance with sub-paragraph (f) of this regulation; and
(f)  ensure that, on the completion of the construction work on each structure comprised in the project, the health and safety file in respect of that structure is delivered to the client.

### GENERAL NOTE

This regulation sets out the duties of the planning supervisor. The exact role of the  **14.02**
planning supervisor will vary from project to project (see Approved Code of Practice, para. 70). In particular, in some projects the role may be facilitative, in ensuring that there is a proper flow of communication at all times on matters relating to design. In other projects when, *e.g.* there are a number of designers involved

(whether professionals or specialist contractors), the planning supervisor will have a co-ordinating function. The planning supervisor will always, however, be under a duty to ensure that the designer has complied with reg. 13(2)(a) and (b) and applied the principles outlined in Approved Code of Practice, para. 56 and to ensure that the health and safety file is prepared (although he does not need to prepare it personally). No format is specified for the health and safety file, but as has been made clear in reg. 12, it must be easy to inspect and store safely. The Approved Code of Practice suggests (App. 5) that since information in the file needs to include that which will assist people carrying out construction work on the structure in the future, the file may include the following details: (1) record or "as built" drawings and plans used and produced throughout the construction process along with the design criteria; (2) general details of the construction methods and materials used; (3) details of the structure's equipment and maintenance facilities; (4) maintenance procedures and requirements for the structure; (5) manuals produced by specialist contractors and suppliers which outline operating and maintenance procedures and schedules for plant and equipment installed as part of the structure; and (6) details on the location and nature of utilities and services, including emergency and fire-fighting systems.

### Derogation

**14.03** This regulation shall not apply, by virtue of reg. 3(2), to construction work in a project if the client has reasonable grounds for believing that the project is not notifiable and the number of people carrying out construction work is less than 5.

**14.04** This regulation also shall not apply, by virtue of reg. 3(8), where construction work in a project is carried out for a domestic client unless the client has made an arrangement with a developer under reg. 5.

**14.05** Reg. 14(b) shall not apply, by virtue of reg. 3(5), to those projects where there is only one designer.

### Practicable and Reasonably Practicable

**14.06** See the comments on distinction between "practicable" and "reasonably practicable" in General Notes to annotations for regs. 6 and 10 (paras. 6.06 and 10.05, above, respectively).

### DEFINITIONS

**14.07** "cleaning work": reg. 2.
"client": reg. 2.
"construction work": reg. 2.
"design": reg. 2.
"designer": reg. 2.
"health and safety file": reg. 2.
"planning supervisor": reg. 2.
"project": reg. 2.
"structure": reg. 2.

**Requirements relating to the health and safety plan**

**15.**—(1)   The planning supervisor appointed for any project shall ensure   **15.01**
that a health and safety plan in respect of the project has been prepared no
later than the time specified in paragraph (2) and contains the information
specified in paragraph (3).

(2)   The time when the health and safety plan is required by paragraph
(1) to be prepared is such time as will enable the health and safety plan to be
provided to any contractor before arrangements are made for the contractor
to carry out or manage construction work.

(3)   The information required by paragraph (1) to be contained in the
health and safety plan is—

(a)   a general description of the construction work comprised in the
project;

(b)   details of the time within which it is intended that the project, and
any intermediate stages, will be completed;

(c)   details of risks to the health or safety of any person carrying out the
construction work so far as such risks are known to the planning
supervisor or are reasonably foreseeable;

(d)   any other information which the planning supervisor knows or could
ascertain by making reasonable enquiries and which it would be
necessary to any contractor to have if he wished to show—

(i)   that he has the competence on which any person is required to
be reasonably satisfied by regulation 8, or

(ii)   that he has allocated or, as appropriate, will allocate adequate
resources on which any person is required to be reasonably
satisfied by regulation 9;

(e)   such information as the planning supervisor knows or could
ascertain by making reasonable enquiries and which it is reasonable
for the planning supervisor to expect the principal contractor to need
in order for him to comply with the requirement imposed on him by
paragraph (4); and

(f)   such information as the planning supervisor knows or could
ascertain by making reasonable enquiries and which it would be
reasonable for any contractor to know in order to understand how he
can comply with any requirements placed upon him in respect of
welfare by or under the relevant statutory provisions.

(4)   The principal contractor shall take such measures as it is reasonable for a person in his position to take to ensure that the health and
safety plan contains until the end of the construction phase the following
features:

(a)   arrangements for the project (including, where necessary for the
management of construction work and monitoring of compliance
with the relevant statutory provisions) which will ensure, so far as is
reasonably practicable, the health and safety of all persons at work

       carrying out the construction work and all persons who may be affected by the work of such persons at work, taking account of—

         (i)   risks involved in the construction work,

         (ii)  any activity specified in paragraph (5); and

  (b)  sufficient information about arrangements for the welfare of persons at work by virtue of the project to enable any contractor to understand how he can comply with any requirements placed upon him in respect of welfare by or under the relevant statutory provisions.

(5)    An activity is an activity referred to in paragraph (4)(a)(ii) if—

  (a)  it is an activity of persons at work; and

  (b)  it is carried out in or on the premises where construction work is or will be carried out; and

  (c)  either—

         (i)   the activity may affect the health or safety of persons at work carrying out the construction work or persons who may be affected by the work of such persons at work, or

         (ii)  the health or safety of the persons at work carrying out the activity may be affected by the work of persons at work carrying out the construction work.

## GENERAL NOTE

**15.02**    The planning supervisor shall ensure that a health and safety plan, which is one of the cornerstones of the regime introduced by these Regulations, is prepared before arrangements are made for any contractor to begin work, and that the principal contractor maintains the health and safety plan in accordance with the Regulations. In practice this means that the health and safety plan must be in a sufficiently advanced state to allow it to be included in any tender documentation. In this way contractors, including a principal contractor, would be able to prepare their tender in such a way as to comply with the health and safety plan—see Approved Code of Practice, para. 77 (see also para. 6.08, above).

**15.03**    The level and amount of information required to be incorporated in the health and safety plan by the planning supervisor will depend on the complexity, size, scope and dangers of the project. It is intended to be project specific. The Approved Code of Practice suggests, at App. 4, that the following may be appropriate considerations when compiling the health and safety plan: (1) nature of project (name of client; location; nature of construction work; and timescale for completion of construction work); (2) existing environment (surrounding land uses and related restrictions; existing services; existing traffic systems and restrictions; existing structures; and ground conditions); (3) existing drawings (available drawings of structures to be demolished or incorporated, which may include an existing health and safety file); (4) design (significant hazards identified by designers which cannot be avoided together with precautions for dealing with them; principles of the structural design and any precautions needed during construction; and detailed reference to specific problems where contractors will be required to explain their proposals for managing these problems); (5) construction materials (health hazards arising from construction materials where particular precautions are required either because of their nature or the manner of their intended use); (6) site-wide elements (positioning of site access and egress points; location of temporary site accommodation; location of unloading, layout and storage areas; and traffic/pedestrian routes); (7) overlap with client's undertaking (consideration of the health and safety issues which arise when the project is to be located in premises occupied or partially occupied by the client); (8) site rules (specific site rules which the client or the planning supervisor may wish to lay down as a result of points(1)–(7) or for other reasons); and (9) continuing liaison (procedures for considering the health and safety implications of design elements of the principal contractor's and other contractors' packages; and procedures for dealing with unforeseen eventualities during the project resulting in substantial design change and which might affect resources).

Once the principal contractor has been appointed the health and safety plan **15.04** should be passed to the principal contractor in order that it can comply with its duties under reg. 15(4). In particular the principal contractor should then develop the health and safety plan in accordance with reg. 15(4)(a) and (b). One aspect of the development of the health and safety plan not explicitly referred to in this regulation, is the incorporation of the whole, or part, of the risk assessment reports required to be produced by each contractor under reg. 19(1)(b) in accordance with the Management of Health and Safety at Work Regulations 1992, reg. 8.

**Changes and Variations**

See the annotations to reg. 10 (para. 10.03, above) on the effect of changes and/or **15.05** variations to the design.

**Derogation**

This regulation shall not apply, by virtue of reg. 3(2), to construction work in a **15.06** project if the client has reasonable grounds for believing that the project is not notifiable and the number of people carrying out construction work is less than 5.

This regulation shall also not apply, by virtue of reg. 3(8), where construction work **15.07** in a project is carried out for a domestic client unless the client has made an arrangement with a developer under reg. 5.

**Practicable and Reasonably Practicable**

See the comments on distinction between "practicable" and "reasonably practi- **15.08** cable" in General Notes to regs. 6 and 10 (paras. 6.06 and 10.05, above, respectively).

**DEFINITIONS**

"construction phase": reg. 2.                     **15.09**
"construction work": reg. 2.
"contractor": reg. 2.
"health and safety plan": reg. 2.
"planning supervisor": reg. 2.
"principal contractor": reg. 2.
"project": reg. 2.

### Requirements on and powers of principal contractor

**16.01**  **16.**—(1)  The principal contractor appointed for any project shall—

(a)  take reasonable steps to ensure co-operation between all contractors (whether they are sharing the construction site for the purposes of regulation 9 of the Management of Health and Safety at Work Regulations 1992**(a)** or otherwise) so far as is necessary to enable each of those contractors to comply with the requirements and prohibitions imposed on him by or under the relevant statutory provisions relating to the construction work;

(b)  ensure, so far as is reasonably practicable, that every contractor, and every employee at work in connection with the project complies with any rules contained in the health and safety plan;

(c)  take reasonable steps to ensure that only authorised persons are allowed into any premises or part of premises where construction work is being carried out;

(d)  ensure that the particulars required to be in any notice under regulation 7 are displayed in a readable condition in a position where they can be read by any person at work on construction work in connection with the project; and

(e)  promptly provide the planning supervisor with any information which—

(i)  is in the possession of the principal contractor or which he could ascertain by making reasonable enquiries of a contractor, and

(ii)  it is reasonable to believe the planning supervisor would include in the health and safety file in order to comply with the requirements imposed on him in respect thereof in regulation 14, and

(iii)  is not in the possession of the planning supervisor.

(2)  The principal contractor may—

(a)  give reasonable directions to any contractor so far as is necessary to enable the principal contractor to comply with his duties under these Regulations;

(b)  include in the health and safety plan rules for the management of the construction work which are reasonably required for the purposes of health and safety.

(3)  Any rules contained in the health and safety plan shall be in writing and shall be brought to the attention of persons who may be affected by them.

---

**(a)**  S.I. 1992/2051.

**GENERAL NOTE**

This regulation sets out the duties of the principal contractor. As already **16.02** mentioned, the principal contractor is appointed by the client (or its agent) and the only restriction on the principal contractor's appointment is that it must be a contractor, it must be competent and it must have allocated adequate resources to enable it to perform its health and safety duties under the Regulations. Having received the health and safety plan from the planning supervisor, the principal contractor shall: (1) ensure the contractors co-operate between themselves in order to enable them to carry out their health and safety obligations under the Regulations, including reg. 9 (Co-operation and co-ordination) of the Management of Health and Safety at Work Regulations 1992 which applies where two or more employers share a work place and requires them to co-ordinate and co-operate with each other in order to comply with their statutory duties; (2) ensure that any contractor and employee complies with rules in the health and safety plans (contractors have a duty under reg. 19(1)(c) to comply with such rules); (3) take reasonable steps to ensure that only authorised people are allowed on site; (4) ensure that particulars of the project given to the Executive by the planning supervisor (reg. 7) are displayed at the site; (5) provide the planning supervisor with such information as is requested; (6) bring any rules in the health and safety plan to the attention of those who may be affected by them and give directions to any contractor in relation to compliance with the Regulations; (7) ensure that there are arrangement for the views of the employees to be expressed in relation to health and safety (though under reg. 18, this is nevertheless a duty of the principal contractor); (8) ensure that information required to be given by statute and any health and safety training required is provided (though given under reg. 17, this is nevertheless a duty of the principal contractor); and (9) ensure that each contractor has comprehensive information on the risks to health and safety to that contractor arising out of the project (again, though given under reg. 17, this is nevertheless a duty of the principal contractor).

The role of the principal contractor is then to evaluate risk in relation to the duties **16.03** of the contractors, to co-ordinate, to manage and to give practical effect to the duties of the contractors. Notwithstanding this duty to co-ordinate, each contractor nevertheless retains its duty under the Management of Health and Safety at Work Regulations 1992, reg. 9.

**Derogation**

This regulation shall not apply, by virtue of reg. 3(2), to construction work in a **16.04** project if the client has reasonable grounds for believing that the project is not notifiable and the number of people carrying out construction work is less than 5.

This regulation shall also not apply, by virtue of reg. 3(8), where construction work **16.05** is carried out for a domestic client unless the client has made an arrangement with a developer under reg. 5.

**Practicable and Reasonably Practicable**

See the comments on distinction between "practicable" and "reasonably practi- **16.06** cable" in General Notes to regs. 6 and 10 (paras. 6.06 and 10.05, above, respectively).

**Regulation 16(1)**   *Contractor*

**16.07**   Reg. 16(1)(a) shall not apply, by virtue of reg. 3(6), to those projects where there is only one contractor. See General Note (paras. 16.02, 16.03, above) in relation to reg. 9 of the Management of Health and Safety at Work Regulations 1992.

### *Subs. (1)(c)*

**16.08**   As with reg. 10 an action for breach of statutory duty may be open in respect of a failure to comply with this regulation, see the General Note to reg. 21 (paras. 21.02–21.10, below). This regulation as with reg. 10, imposes a standard of reasonable practicability, see the General Notes to regs. 6 and 10 (paras. 6.06 and 10.05, above, respectively).

## DEFINITIONS

**16.09**   "construction work": reg. 2.
"contractor": reg. 2.
"health and safety file": reg. 2.
"health and safety plan": reg. 2.
"planning supervisor": reg. 2.
"principal contractor": reg. 2.
"project": reg. 2.

## Information and training

**17.**—(1)  The principal contractor appointed for any project shall ensure, **17.01**
so far as is reasonably practicable, that every contractor is provided with
comprehensible information on the risks to the health or safety of that
contractor or of any employees or other persons under the control of that
contractor arising out of or in connection with the construction work.

(2)  The principal contractor shall ensure, so far as is reasonably
practicable, that every contractor who is an employer provides any of his
employees at work carrying out the construction work with—
  (a)  any information which the employer is required to provide to those
       employees in respect of that work by virtue of regulation 8 of the
       Management of Health and Safety at Work Regulations 1992; and
  (b)  any health and safety training which the employer is required to
       provide to those employees in respect of that work by virtue of
       regulation 11(2)(b) of the Management of Health and Safety at
       Work Regulations 1992.

### GENERAL NOTE

The principal contractor shall ensure that each contractor has comprehensive **17.02**
information as to the risks to health and safety to that contractor arising out of the
project and that information required to be given by statute and any health and safety
training is provided. Such information as is given should be included within the
health and safety plan and, if not given at tender stage, should be given as soon as it
becomes available, thus allowing contractors to comply with reg. 9(3). The
Management of Health and Safety at Work Regulations 1992, reg. 8 (Information for
employees) provides that employers are to provide employees with "comprehensible
and relevant" information concerning risks identified by assessments, preventative
and protective measures, procedures for serious and imminent danger and the name
of the person to implement such procedures, and any risks notified to the employer
by other employers on the site in connection with their particular undertaking. The
Management of Health and Safety at Work Regulations 1992, reg. 11(2)(b), provides
that employers are to ensure that their employees receive adequate training when
they are being exposed to new or increased risks due to: (1) a transfer or change of
responsibility; (2) the introduction of new, or change of existing, work equipment or
technology; or (3) the introduction of new, or a change of an existing, system of work.

### Derogation

This regulation shall not apply, by virtue of reg. 3(2), to construction work in a **17.03**
project if the client has reasonable grounds for believing that the project is not
notifiable and the number of people carrying out construction work is less than 5.

This regulation also shall not apply, by virtue of reg. 3(8), where construction work **17.04**
in a project is carried out for a domestic client unless the client has made an
arrangement with a developer under reg. 5.

**Practicable and Reasonably Practicable**

**17.05**     See the comments on distinction between "practicable" and "reasonably practicable" in General Notes to annotations for regs. 6 and 10 (paras. 6.06 and 10.05, above, respectively).

**DEFINITIONS**

**17.06**     "construction work": reg. 2.
"contractor": reg. 2.
"principal contractor": reg. 2.
"project": reg. 2.

**Advice from, and views of, persons at work**

**18.** The principal contractor shall—  **18.01**
(a) ensure that employees and self-employed persons at work on the construction work are able to discuss, and offer advice to him on, matters connected with the project which it can reasonably be foreseen will affect their health or safety; and
(b) ensure that there are arrangements for the co-ordination of the views of employees at work on construction work or of their representatives, where necessary for reasons of health and safety having regard to the nature of the construction work and the size of the premises where the construction work is being carried out.

## GENERAL NOTE

This regulation provides that arrangements should be made for the views of  **18.02**
employees and the self-employed to be expressed in relation to health and safety and to be co-ordinated. This mechanism is intended to provide a conduit for any on site comments which individuals may have. There already exists under the Safety Representatives and Safety Committees Regulations 1977 (S.I. 1977 No. 500) the mechanism for representatives to be appointed by recognised trades unions, and where such a representative is appointed this regulation effectively backs up the employers duty under the 1977 Regulations to consult such a representative.

### Derogation

This regulation shall not apply, by virtue of reg. 3(2), to construction work in a  **18.03**
project if the client has reasonable grounds for believing that the project is not notifiable and the number of people carrying out construction work is less than 5.

This regulation also shall not apply, by virtue of reg. 3(8), where construction work  **18.04**
in a project is carried out for a domestic client unless the client has made an arrangement with a developer under reg. 5.

## DEFINITIONS

"construction work": reg. 2.  **18.05**
"principal contractor": reg. 2.
"project": reg. 2.

**Requirements and prohibitions on contractors**

**19.01**  **19.**—(1)  Every contractor shall, in relation to the project—

(a)  co-operate with the principal contractor so far as is necessary to enable each of them to comply with his duties under the relevant statutory provisions;

(b)  so far as is reasonably practicable, promptly provide the principal contractor with any information (including any relevant part of any risk assessment in his possession or control made by virtue of the Management of Health and Safety at Work Regulations 1992) which might affect the health or safety of any person at work carrying out the construction work or of any person who may be affected by the work of such a person at work or which might justify a review of the health and safety plan;

(c)  comply with any directions of the principal contractor given to him under regulation 16(2)(a);

(d)  comply with any rules applicable to him in the health and safety plan;

(e)  promptly provide the principal contractor with the information in relation to any death, injury, condition or dangerous occurrence which the contractor is required to notify or report by virtue of the Reporting of Injuries, Diseases and Dangerous Occurrences Regulations 1985**(a)**; and

(f)  promptly provide the principal contractor with any information which—

  (i)  is in the possession of the contractor or which he could ascertain by making reasonable enquiries of persons under his control, and

  (ii)  it is reasonable to believe the principal contractor would provide to the planning supervisor in order to comply with the requirements imposed on the principal contractor in respect thereof by regulation 16(1)(e), and

  (iii)  which is not in the possession of the said principal contractor.

(2)  No employer shall cause or permit any employee of his to work on contruction work unless the employer has been provided with the information mentioned in paragraph (4).

(3)  No self-employed person shall work on construction work unless he has been provided with the information mentioned in paragraph (4).

(4)  The information referred to in paragraphs (2) and (3) is—

(a)  the name of the planning supervisor for the project;

(b)  the name of the principal contractor for the project;

(c)  the contents of the health and safety plan or such part of it as is relevant to the construction work which any such employee or, as the case may be, which the self-employed person, is to carry out.

---

**(a)**  S.I. 1985/2023.

(5) It shall be a defence in any proceedings for contravention of paragraph (2) or (3) for the employer or self-employed person to show that he made all reasonable enquiries and reasonably believed—

(a) that he had been provided with the information mentioned in paragraph (4); or

(b) that, by virtue of any provision in regulation 3, this regulation did not apply to the construction work.

## GENERAL NOTE

This regulation ensures that the requirements placed on the contractors under this regulation complement the duties placed on the principal contractor in regulation 16. **19.02**

### Derogation

This regulation shall not apply, by virtue of reg. 3(2), to construction work in a project if the client has reasonable grounds for believing that the project is not notifiable and the number of people carrying out construction work is less than 5. **19.03**

This regulation shall also not apply, by virtue of reg. 3(8), where construction work in a project is carried out for a domestic client unless the client has made an arrangement with a developer under reg. 5. **19.04**

### Practicable and Reasonably Practicable

See the comments on distinction between "practicable" and "reasonably practicable" in General Notes to annotations for regs. 6 and 10 (paras. 6.06 and 10.05, above, respectively). **19.05**

### Regulation 19(5)

See General Note on Criminal implications of the Regulations (paras. 1.21 to 1.28, above. **19.06**

## DEFINITIONS

"construction work": reg. 2. **19.07**
"contractor": reg. 2.
"health and safety plan": reg. 2.
"planning supervisor": reg. 2.
"principal contractor": reg. 2.
"project": reg. 2.

### Extension outside Great Britain

**20.01**    **20.**    These regulations shall apply to any activity to which sections 1 to 59 and 80 to 82 of the Health and Safety at Work etc. Act 1974 apply by virtue of article 7 of the Health and Safety at Work etc. Act 1974 (Application outside Great Britain) Order 1989**(a)** other than the activities specified in sub-paragraphs (b), (c) and (d) of that article as they apply to any such activity in Great Britain.

**GENERAL NOTE**

**20.02**    The Health and Safety at Work etc. Act 1974 (Application outside Great Britain) Order 1989 has now been revoked and replaced by the Health and Safety at Work etc. Act 1974 (Application outside Great Britain) Order 1995, S.I. 1995 No. 263, which came into force on March 15, 1995.

---

**(a)**   S.I. 1989/840.

## Exclusion of civil liability

**21.**   Breach of a duty imposed by these Regulations, other than those   **21.01**
imposed by regulation 10 and regulation 16(1)(c), shall not confer a right of
action in any civil proceedings.

## GENERAL NOTE

By virtue of reg. 21 civil liability for breach of any duty imposed by the Regulations   **21.02**
is excluded, except in relation to regs. 10 and 16(1)(c).

### Breach of Statutory Duty

The exclusion of liability relates only to cases in respect of what is known as breach   **21.03**
of statutory duty. A full examination of the concept of breach of statutory duty is
beyond the scope of this commentary, but for present purposes it may be observed
that for an action based on breach of statutory duty three matters require to be
present,

First, there requires to be a statutory provision (in the present case either reg. 10 or   **21.04**
reg. 16(1)(c)) which imposes upon a party, who is the defendant (defender in
Scotland) in the action, a duty which is intended to occasion an element of protection
to persons such as the plaintiff (pursuer in Scotland) in the action: see *e.g. Gallagher
v. Wimpey & Co. Ltd* 1951 S.C. 515. The plaintiff/pursuer must be one of the category
of persons to whom it was intended to afford protection: see *Hartley v. Mayo & Co.*
[1954] 1 Q.B. 383.

Secondly, the plaintiff/pursuer will require to show that the defendant/defender   **21.05**
failed to perform the duty incumbent upon him. That, in turn, requires an
examination of (1) the standard of duty, and (2) the breach of duty by failing to meet
the requisite standard. The standard of duty is determined by the wording of the
provision. It may impose upon the defendant/defender the obligation "to ensure"
that something is done. Alternatively, the obligation may be to do something insofar
as it is "reasonably practicable" or, separately, insofar as it is "practicable" (see the
General Note to regs. 6 and 10—paras. 6.06 and 10.05, above, respectively—in
respect of "practicable" and "reasonably practicable"). The extent to which the
standard has not been met will be a matter of fact and circumstance in each instance.

Lastly, the plaintiff/pursuer must establish that the breach of duty causing injury to   **21.06**
the plaintiff/pursuer was of the type that the statutory provision was designed to
protect against, see, *e.g. Gorris v. Scott* (1874) L.R. 9 Ex. 125 (or the Scottish case of
*Grant v. N.C.B.* 1956 S.C.(H.L.) 48). The plaintiff/pursuer must also, of course,
establish that the breach of duty caused, or materially contributed to, the injuries
sustained by him.

Reg. 21 is necessary due to the terms of the Health and Safety at Work etc. Act   **21.07**
1974, s.47(2), which provides that a breach of a duty imposed by *inter alia* health and
safety regulations (which the Regulations are) will be actionable unless the
regulations provide otherwise. The Regulations are drafted in such a way that the
remedy of breach of statutory duty is only available in respect of regs. 10 and 16(1)(c).

### Negligence

**21.08**    As observed above, the exclusion provided for by reg. 21 only applies to actions for a breach of statutory duty. In the law of tort (delict in Scotland) a party may also commence proceedings based upon the common law of negligence. To succeed in an action a plaintiff/pursuer, in general terms, must establish (1) that the defendant/defender owed to the plaintiff/pursuer a duty of care for the safety of his person or property, (2) that the defendant/defender was in breach of that duty, and (3) that the breach of duty occasioned harm to the plaintiff/pursuer's person or property.

**21.09**    A crucial question that will arise in actions at common law will be what is the standard of care? It may well be successfully argued by a plaintiff/pursuer that the Regulations set out what is the common law standard of care. Such an approach has been taken by the courts in respect of the Control of Lead at Work Regulations 1980 (S.I. 1980 No. 1248) and their accompanying Approved Code of Practice, see *Hewett v. Alf Brown's Transport Ltd* [1991] I.C.R. 471. See also *Butt v. Inner London Education Authority* [1986] 66 L.G.R. 379, in which the Court of Appeal upheld a county court judgment which had regard to the provisions of the Factories Acts notwithstanding that the premises in question were a school.

**21.10**    There is every likelihood that the courts will view the Regulations in a similar manner and hold that a party failing to comply with the terms of the Regulations has not met the appropriate standard of care. However, it will be a question of fact in each case as to whether the statutory duty is more or less co-extensive with the common law duty.

### Approved Code of Practice

**21.11**    See also commentary above in respect of the legal status of the Approved Code of Practice, at paras. 1.14 to 1.20, above, and in respect of reg. 10 (paras. 10.02–10.04, above) and reg. 16(1)(c) (para. 16.08, above).

**Enforcement**

**22.** Notwithstanding regulation 3 of the Health and Safety (Enforcing **22.01** Authority) Regulations 1989**(b)**, the enforcing authority for these Regulations shall be the Executive.

**GENERAL NOTE**

See also General Note to reg. 3 (paras. 3.02–3.09, above). **22.02**

**Transitional provisions**

**23.** Schedule 2 shall have effect with respect to projects which have **23.01** started, but the construction phase of which has not ended, when these Regulations come into force.

---

**(b)** S.I. 1989/1903.

### Repeals, revocations and modifications

**24.01**   **24.**—(1)   Subsections (6) and (7) of section 127 of the Factories Act 1961**(c)** are repealed.

(2)   Regulations 5 and 6 of the Construction (General Provisions) Regulations 1961**(d)** are revoked.

(3)   The Construction (Notice of Operations and Works) Order 1965**(e)** is revoked.

(4)   For item (i) of paragraph 4(a) of Schedule 2 to the Health and Safety (Enforcing Authority) Regulations 1989, the following item shall be substituted—

"(i)   regulation 7(1) of the Construction (Design and Management) Regulations 1994 (S.I. 1994/3140) (which requires projects which include or are intended to include construction work to be notified to the Executive) applies to the project which includes the work; or".

### GENERAL NOTE

#### Regulation 24(4)

**24.02**   This replaces a reference to the Factories Act 1961, s.127(6), which required certain works to be notified to an inspector.

Signed by order of the Secretary of State

*Philip Oppenheim*
Parliamentary Under Secretary of State
Department of Employment

19th December 1994

---

**(c)**   1961 c. 34.
**(d)**   S.I. 1961/1580: to which there are amendments not relevant to these Regulations.
**(e)**   S.I. 1965/221.

SCHEDULE 1 **Regulation 7 25.01**

## PARTICULARS TO BE NOTIFIED TO THE EXECUTIVE

1. Date of forwarding.
2. Exact address of the construction site.
3. Name and address of the client or clients (see note).
4. Type of project.
5. Name and address of the planning supervisor.
6. A declaration signed by or on behalf of the planning supervisor that he has been appointed as such.
7. Name and address of the principal contractor.
8. A declaration signed by or on behalf of the principal contractor that he has been appointed as such.
9. Date planned for start of the construction phase.
10. Planned duration of the construction phase.
11. Estimated maximum number of people at work on the construction site.
12. Planned number of contractors on the construction site.
13. Name and address of any contractor or contractors already chosen.

Note: Where a declaration has been made in accordance with regulation 4(4), item 3 above refers to the client or clients on the basis that that declaration has not yet taken effect.

**26.01**                             SCHEDULE 2                      **Regulation 23**


## TRANSITIONAL PROVISIONS


1.   Until 1st January 1996, regulation 6 shall not apply in respect of a project the construction phase of which started before the coming into force of these Regulations.

2.   Where at the coming into force of these Regulations the time specified in regulation 6(3) for the appointment of the planning supervisor has passed, the time for appointing the planning supervisor by virtue of regulation 6(1)(a) shall be as soon as is practicable after the coming into force of these Regulations.

3.   Where at the coming into force of these Regulations the time specified in regulations 6(4) for the appointment of the principal contractor has passed, the time for appointing the principal contractor by virtue of regulation 6(1)(b) shall be as soon as is practicable after the coming into force of these Regulations.

4.   Regulation 7 shall not require notification of any project where notice of all construction work included in the project has been given in accordance with section 127(6) of the Factories Act 1961 before the coming into force of these Regulations.

5.   Regulation 10 shall not apply to any project the construction phase of which starts before 1st August 1995.

6.   Regulation 11 shall not apply to any project the construction phase of which started before the coming into force of these Regulations.

7.   Until 1st August 1995, regulation 13 and regulation 14(a) shall not apply in respect of any design the preparation of which started before the coming into force of these Regulations.

# APPENDICES

## Appendix 1

(The Temporary or Mobile Construction Sites Directive)

### COUNCIL DIRECTIVE 92/57/EEC
of 24 June 1992
on the implementation of minimum safety and health requirements at temporary or mobile constructions sites (eighth individual Directive within the meaning of Article 16 (1) of Directive 89/391/EEC)

THE COUNCIL OF THE EUROPEAN COMMUNITIES,

Having regard to the Treaty establishing the European Economic Community, **A1.01** and in particular Article 118a thereof,

Having regard to the proposal from the Commission([1]), submitted after consulting the Advisory Committee on Safety, Hygiene and Health Protection at Work,

In cooperation with the European Parliament([2]),

Having regard to the opinion of the Economic and Social Committee([3]),

Whereas Article 118a of the Treaty provides that the Council shall adopt, by means of directives, minimum requirements for encouraging improvements, especially in the working environment, to ensure a better level of protection of the safety and health of workers;

Whereas, under the terms of that Article, those directives are to avoid imposing administrative, financial and legal constraints in a way which would hold back the creation and development of small and medium-sized undertakings;

Whereas the communication from the Commission on its programme concerning safety, hygiene and health at work([4]) provides for the adoption of a Directive designed to guarantee the safety and health of workers at temporary or mobile construction sites;

Whereas, in its resolution of 21 December 1987 on safety, hygiene and health at work([5]), the Council took note of the Commission's intention of submitting to the Council in the near future minimum requirements concerning temporary or mobile construction sites;

Whereas temporary or mobile construction sites constitute an area of activity that exposes workers to particularly high levels of risk;

Whereas unsatisfactory architectural and/or organizational options or poor planning of the works at the project preparation stage have played a role in more than half of the occupational accidents occurring on construction sites in the Community;

Whereas in each Member State the authorities responsible for safety and health at work must be informed, before the beginning of the works, of the execution of works the scale of which exceeds a certain threshold;

Whereas, when a project is being carried out, a large number of occupational accidents may be caused by inadequate coordination, particularly where various undertakings work simultaneously or in succession at the same temporary or mobile construction site;

Whereas it is therefore necessary to improve coordination between the various parties concerned at the project preparation stage and also when the work is being carried out;

Whereas compliance with the minimum requirements designed to guarantee a

---

([1]) O.J. No. C.213, 28.8.1990, p. 2 and O.J. No. C.112, 27.4.1991, p. 4.
([2]) O.J. No. C.78, 18.3.1990, p. 172 and O.J. No. C.150, 15.6.1992.
([3]) O.J. No. C.120, 6.5.1991, p. 24.
([4]) O.J. No. C.28, 3.2.1988, p. 3.
([5]) O.J. No. C.28, 3.2.1988, p. 1.

better standard of safety and health at temporary or mobile construction sites is essential to ensure the safety and health of workers;

Whereas, moreover, self-employed persons and employers, where they are personally engaged in work activity, may, through their activities on a temporary or mobile construction site, jeopardize the safety and health of workers;

Whereas it is therefore necessary to extend to self-employed persons and to employers where they are personally engaged in work activity on the site certain relevant provisions of Council Directive 89/655/EEC of 30 November 1989 concerning the minimum safety and health requirements for the use of work equipment by workers at work (second individual Directive)([6]), and of Council Directive 89/656/EEC of 30 November 1989 on the minimum health and safety requirements for the use by workers of personal protective equipment at the workplace (third individual Directive)([7]);

Whereas this Directive is an individual Directive within the meaning of Article 16(1) of Council Directive 89/391/EEC of 12 June 1989 on the introduction of measures to encourage improvements in the safety and health of workers at work([8]); whereas, therefore, the provisions of the said Directive are fully applicable to temporary or mobile construction sites, without prejudice to more stringent and/or specific provisions contained in this Directive;

Whereas this Directive constitutes a practical step towards the achievement of the social dimension of the internal market with special reference to the subject matter of Council Directive 89/106/EEC of 21 December 1988 on the approximation of laws, regulations and administrative provisions of the Member States relating to construction products([9]) and the subject matter covered by Council Directive 89/440/EEC of 18 July 1989 amending Directive 71/305/EEC concerning coordination of procedures for the award of public work contracts([10]);

Whereas, pursuant to Council Decision 74/325/EEC([11]), the Advisory Committee on Safety, Hygiene and Health Protection at Work is consulted by the Commission with a view to drawing up proposals in this field,

HAS ADOPTED THIS DIRECTIVE:

*Article 1*

**Subject**

**A1.02**    1. This Directive, which is the eighth individual Directive within the meaning of Article 16(1) of Directive 89/391/EEC, lays down minimum safety and health requirements for temporary or mobile construction sites, as defined in Article 2(a).

2. This Directive shall not apply to drilling and extraction in the extractive industries within the meaning of Article 1(2) of Council Decision 74/326/EEC of 27 June 1974 on the extension of the responsibilities of the Mines Safety and Health Commission to all mineral-extracting industries([12]).

3. The provisions of Directive 89/391/EEC are fully applicable to the whole scope referred to in paragraph 1, without prejudice to more stringent and/or specific provisions contained in this Directive.

---

([6]) O.J. No. L.393, 30.12.1989, p. 13.
([7]) O.J. No. L.393, 30.12.1989, p. 18.
([8]) O.J. No. L.183, 29.6.1989, p.1.
([9]) O.J. No. L.40, 11.2.1989, p. 12.
([10]) O.J. No. L.210, 21.7.1989, p. 1. Amended by Commission Decision 90/380/EEC (O.J. No. L.187, 19.7.1990, p. 55).
([11]) O.J. No. L.185, 9.7.1974, p.15. Last amended by the 1985 Act of Accession.
([12]) O.J. No. L.185, 9.7.1974, p. 18.

## Article 2

### Definitions

For the purposes of this Directive:  A1.03
(a)  'temporary or mobile construction sites' (hereinafter referred to as 'construction sites') means any construction site at which building or civil engineering works are carried out; a non-exhaustive list of such works is given in Annex I;
(b)  'client' means any natural or legal person for whom a project is carried out;
(c)  'project supervisor' means any natural or legal person responsible for the design and/or execution and/or supervision of the execution of a project, acting on behalf of the client;
(d)  'self-employed person' means any person other than those referred to in Article 3 (a) and (b) of Directive 89/391/EEC whose professional activity contributes to the completion of a project;
(e)  'coordinator for safety and health matters at the project preparations stage' means any natural or legal person entrusted by the client and/or project supervisor, during preparation of the project design, with performing the duties referred to in Article 5;
(f)  'coordinator for safety and health matters at the project execution stage' means any natural or legal person entrusted by the client and/or project supervisor, during execution of the project, with performing the duties referred to in Article 6.

## Article 3

### Appointment of coordinators—Safety and health plan—Prior notice

1. The client or the project supervisor shall appoint one or more coordinators for  A1.04
safety and health matters, as defined in Article 2(e) and (f), for any construction site on which more than one contractor is present.
2. The client or the project supervisor shall ensure that prior to the setting up of a construction site a safety and health plan is drawn up in accordance with Article 5(b).
The Member States may, after consulting both management and the workforce, allow derogations from the provisions of the first paragraph, except where the work concerned involves particular risks as listed in Annex II.
3. In the case of constructions sites:
— on which work is scheduled to last longer than 30 working days and on which more than 20 workers are occupied simultaneously, or
— on which the volume of work is scheduled to exceed 500 person-days,
the client or the project supervisor shall communicate a prior notice drawn up in accordance with Annex III to the competent authorities before work starts.
The prior notice must be clearly displayed on the construction site and, if necessary, periodically updated.

## Article 4

### Project preparation stage: general principles

The project supervisor, or where appropriate the client, shall take account of the  A1.05
general principles of prevention concerning safety and health referred to in Directive 89/391/EEC during the various stages of designing and preparing the project, in particular:
— when architectural, technical and/or organizational aspects are being decided, in order to plan the various items or stages of work which are to take place simultaneously or in succession,

— when estimating the period required for completing such work or work stages. Account shall also be taken, each time this appears necessary, of all safety and health plans and of files drawn up in accordance with Article 5(b) or (c) or adjusted in accordance with Article 6(c).

*Article 5*

**Project preparation stage: duties of coordinators**

**A1.06**     The coordinator(s) for safety and health matters during the project preparation stage appointed in accordance with Article 3(1) shall:

(a)    coordinate implementation of the provisions of Article 4;

(b)    draw up, or cause to be drawn up, a safety and health plan setting out the rules applicable to the construction site concerned, taking into account where necessary the industrial activities taking place on the site; this plan must also include specific measures concerning work which falls within one or more of the categories of Annex II;

(c)    prepare a file appropriate to the characteristics of the project containing relevant safety and health information to be taken into account during any subsequent works.

*Article 6*

**Project execution stage: duties of coordinators**

**A1.07**     The coordinator(s) for safety and health matters during the project execution stage appointed in accordance with Article 3(1) shall:

(a)    coordinate implementation of the general principles of prevention and safety:
— when technical and/or organizational aspects are being decided, in order to plan the various items or stages of work which are to take place simultaneously or in succession,
— when estimating the period required for completing such work or work stages;

(b)    coordinate implementation of the relevant provisions in order to ensure that employers and, if necessary for the protection of workers, self-employed persons:
— apply the principles referred to in Article 8 in a consistent manner,
— where required, follow the safety and health plan referred to in Article 5(b);

(c)    make, or cause to be made, any adjustments required to the safety and health plan referred to in Article 5(b) and the file referred to in Article 5(c) to take account of the progress of the work and any changes which have occurred;

(d)    organize cooperation between employers, including successive employers on the same site, coordination of their activities with a view to protecting workers and preventing accidents and occupational health hazards and reciprocal information as provided for in Article 6(4) of Directive 89/391/EEC, ensuring that self-employed persons are brought into this process where necessary;

(e)    coordinate arrangements to check that the working procedures are being implemented correctly;

(f)    take the steps necessary to ensure that only authorized person are allowed onto the construction site.

*Article 7*

**Responsibilities of clients, project supervisors and employers**

1. Where a client or project supervisor has appointed a coordinator or coordinators **A1.08** to perform the duties referred to in Articles 5 and 6, this does not relieve the client or project supervisor of his responsibilities in that respect.

2. The implementation of Articles 5 and 6, and of paragraph 1 of this Article shall not affect the principle of employers' responsibility as provided for in Directive 89/391/EEC.

*Article 8*

**Implementation of Article 6 of Directive 89/391/EEC**

When the work is being carried out, the principles set out in Article 6 of Directive **A1.09** 89/391/EEC shall be applied, in particular as regards:

(a)  keeping the construction site in good order and in a satisfactory state of cleanliness;

(b)  choosing the location of workstations bearing in mind how access to these workplaces is obtained, and determining routes or areas for the passage and movement and equipment;

(c)  the conditions under which various materials are handled;

(d)  technical maintenance, pre-commissioning checks and regular checks on installations and equipment with a view to correcting any faults which might affect the safety and health of workers;

(e)  the demarcation and laying-out of areas for the storage of various materials, in particular where dangerous materials or substances are concerned;

(f)  the conditions under which the dangerous materials used are removed;

(g)  the storage and disposal or removal of waste and debris;

(h)  the adaptation, based on progress made with the site, of the actual period to be allocated for the various types of work or work stages;

(i)  cooperation between employers and self-employed persons;

(j)  interaction with industrial activities at the place within which or in the vicinity of which the construction site is located.

*Article 9*

**Obligations of employers**

In order to preserve safety and health on the construction site, under the **A1.10** conditions set out in Article 6 and 7, employers shall:

(a)  in particular when implementing Article 8, take measures that are in line with the minimum requirements set out in Annex IV;

(b)  take into account directions from the coordinator(s) for safety and health matters.

*Article 10*

**Obligations of other groups of persons**

1. In order to preserve safety and health on the construction site, self-employed **A1.11** persons shall:

(a)  comply in particular with the following, *mutatis mutandis*:

   (i)  the requirements of Article 6 (4) and Article 13 of Directive 89/391/EEC and Article 8 and Annex IV of this Directive;

   (ii)  Article 4 of Directive 89/655/EEC and the relevant provisions of the Annex thereto;

     (iii)   Article 3, Article 4 (1) to (4) and (9) and Article 5 of Directive 89/656/EEC;

(b)   take into account directions from the coordinator(s) for safety and health matters.

2. In order to preserve safety and health on the site, where employers are personally engaged in work activity on the construction site, they shall:

(a)   comply in particular with the following, *mutatis mutandis*:

     (i)   Article 13 of Directive 89/391/EEC;

     (ii)   Article 4 of Directive 89/655/EEC and the relevant provisions of the Annex thereto;

     (iii)   Articles 3, 4(1), (2), (3), (4), (9) and 5 of Directive 89/656/EEC;

(b)   take account of the comments of the coordinator(s) for safety and health.

## Article 11

### Information for workers

**A1.12**    1. Without prejudice to Article 10 of Directive 89/391/EEC, workers and/or their representatives shall be informed of all the measures to be taken concerning their safety and health on the construction site.

2. The information must be comprehensible to the workers concerned.

## Article 12

### Consultation and participation of workers

**A1.13**    Consultation and participation of workers and/or of their representatives shall take place in accordance with Article 11 of Directive 89/391/EEC on matters covered by Articles 6, 8 and 9 of this Directive, ensuring whenever necessary proper coordination between workers and/or workers' representatives in undertakings carrying out their activities at the workplace, having regard to the degree of risk and the size of the work site.

## Article 13

### Amendment of the Annexes

**A1.14**    1. Amendments to Annexes I, II and III shall be adopted by the Council in accordance with the procedure laid down in Article 118a of the Treaty.

2. Strictly technical adaptations of Annex IV as a result of:

—   the adoption of directives on technical harmonization and standardization regarding temporary or mobile construction sites, and/or

—   technical progress, changes in international regulations or specifications or knowledge in the field of temporary or mobile construction sites

shall be adopted in accordance with the procedure laid down in Article 17 of Directive 89/391/EEC.

## Article 14

### Final provisions

**A1.15**    1. Member States shall bring into force the laws, regulations and administrative provisions necessary to comply with this Directive by 31 December 1993 at the latest. They shall forthwith inform the Commission thereof.

2. When Member States adopt these measures, they shall contain a reference to this Directive or be accompanied by such reference on the occasion of their official publication. The methods of making such a reference shall be laid down by the Member States.

3. Member States shall communicate to the Commission the texts of the provisions of national law which they have already adopted or adopt in the field governed by this Directive.

4. Member States shall report to the Commission every four years on the practical implementation of the provisions of this Directive, indicating the points of view of employers and workers.

The Commission shall inform the European Parliament, the Council, the Economic and Social Committee and the Advisory Committee on Safety, Hygiene and Health Protection at Work.

5. The Commission shall submit periodically to the European Parliament, the Council and the Economic and Social Committee a report on the implementation of this Directive, taking into account paragraphs 1, 2, 3 and 4.

*Article 15*

This Directive is addressed to the Member States.                              **A1.16**

Done at Luxembourg, 24 June 1992.

*For the Council*
*The President*
José da SILVA PENEDA

*ANNEX I*                              **A1.17**

### NON-EXHAUSTIVE LIST OF BUILDING AND CIVIL ENGINEERING WORKS REFERRED TO IN ARTICLE 2(a) OF THE DIRECTIVE

1. Excavation
2. Earthworks
3. Construction
4. Assembly and dissassembly of prefabricated elements
5. Conversion or fitting-out
6. Alterations
7. Renovation
8. Repairs
9. Dismantling
10. Demolition
11. Upkeep
12. Maintenance—Painting and cleaning work
13. Drainage

*ANNEX II*                              **A1.18**

### NON-EXHAUSTIVE LIST OF WORK INVOLVING PARTICULAR RISKS TO THE SAFETY AND HEALTH OF WORKERS REFERRED TO IN ARTICLE 3(2), SECOND PARAGRAPH OF THE DIRECTIVE

1. Work which puts workers at risk of burial under earthfalls, engulfment in swampland or falling from a height, where the risk is particularly aggravated by the nature of the work or processes used or by the environment at the place of work or site[13].
2. Work which puts workers at risk from chemical or biological substances constituting a particular danger to the safety and health of workers or involving a legal requirement for health monitoring.

---

[13] In implementing point 1, Member States have the option of setting figures for individual situations.

3. Work with ionizing radiation requiring the designation of controlled or supervised areas as defined in Article 20 of Directive 80/836/Euratom([14]).
4. Work near high voltage power lines.
5. Work exposing workers to the risk of drowning.
6. Work on wells, underground earthworks and tunnels.
7. Work carried out by drivers having a system of air supply.
8. Work carried out by workers in caisson with a compressed-air atmosphere.
9. Work involving the use of explosives.
10. Work involving the assembly or dismantling of heavy prefabricated components.

**A1.19**

## *ANNEX III*

### CONTENT OF THE PRIOR NOTICE REFERRED TO IN ARTICLE 3(3), FIRST PARAGRAPH OF THE DIRECTIVE I

1. Date of forwarding: ............................................................................................

2. Exact address of the construction site: ...............................................................

   ............................................................................................................................

3. Client(s) (name(s) and address(es)): .................................................................

   ............................................................................................................................

4. Type of project: .................................................................................................

5. Project supervisor(s) (name(s) and address(es)): ..............................................

   ............................................................................................................................

6. Safety and health coordinators(s) during the project preparation stage (name(s))

   and address(es)): ................................................................................................

   ............................................................................................................................

7. Coordinator(s) for safety and health matters during the project execution stage

   (name(s) and address(es)): .................................................................................

   ............................................................................................................................

   ............................................................................................................................

8. Date planned for start of work on the construction site: ...................................

---

([14]) O.J. No. L.246, 17.9.1980, p. 1. Last amended by Directive 84/467/Euratom (O.J. No. L.265, 5.10.1984, p. 4).

9. Planned duration of work on the construction site: ...........................................

10. Estimated maximum number of workers on the construction site: ...................

11. Planned number of contractors and self-employed persons on the construction
    site: ...............................................................................................................
    ........................................................................................................................

12. Details of contractors already chosen: ...............................................................
    ........................................................................................................................
    ........................................................................................................................
    ........................................................................................................................
    ........................................................................................................................

# Appendix 2

(Diagram from HSC "Guide to managing health and safety in construction")

## When do the Regulations apply?

**A2.01**

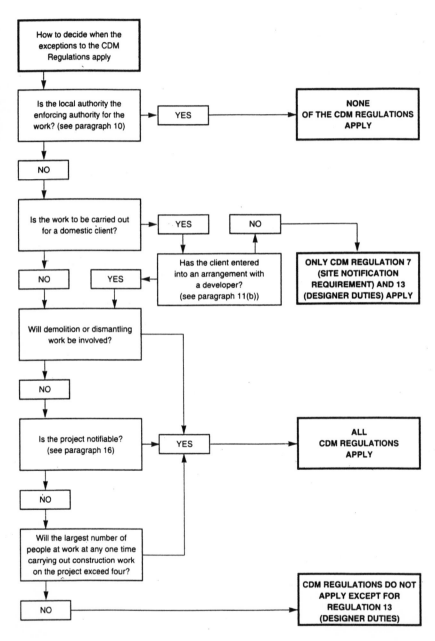

## Appendix 3

(Diagram from HSC "Guide to managing health and safety in construction")

### When is a project notifiable?

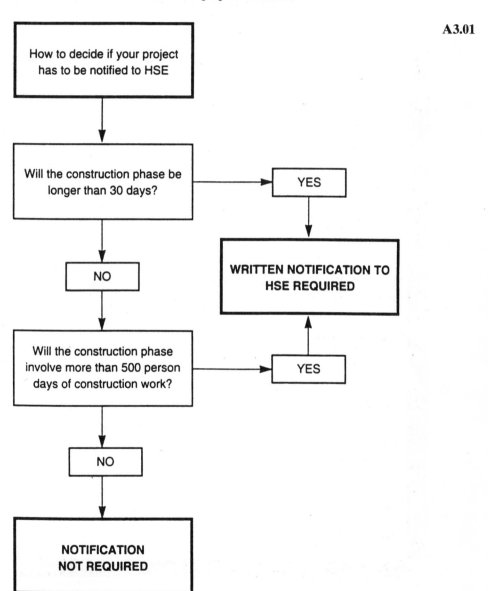

A3.01

How to decide if your project has to be notified to HSE

Will the construction phase be longer than 30 days?

YES

NO

WRITTEN NOTIFICATION TO HSE REQUIRED

Will the construction phase involve more than 500 person days of construction work?

YES

NO

NOTIFICATION NOT REQUIRED

(Appendix 6 from HSC "Guide to managing health and safety in construction")

## A4.01 REQUIREMENTS OF THE CDM REGULATIONS AT THE MAIN STAGES OF A CONSTRUCTION PROJECT

**Stages:** CONCEPT AND FEASIBILITY | DESIGN AND PLANNING | TENDER/SELECTION STAGE | CONSTRUCTION PHASE | COMMISSIONING AND HANDOVER

### CLIENT

**Concept and feasibility / Design and planning:**

- Appoint planning supervisor (regulation 6(1)(a))
- Planning supervisor to be competent and have made adequate provision for health and safety (regulations 8(1) and 9(1))
- Provide planning supervisor with relevant information (regulation 11)
- Ensure that when arranging for any designer(s) to prepare a design, they are competent and have made adequate provision for health and safety (regulations 8(2) and 9(2))
- Ensure notification is submitted to HSE (regulations 7(1) and 7(3))

**Tender/selection stage:**

- Appoint principal contractor (regulation 6(1)(b))
- Principal contractor to be competent and have made adequate provision for health and safety (regulations 8(3) and 9(3))
- Ensure further notification details which were not known at the time of appointment are sent to HSE (regulation 7(4))

**Construction phase:**

- Ensure that when arranging for any contractor(s) to carry out or manage construction work, they are competent and have made adequate provision for health and safety (regulations 8(3) and 9(3))
- Comply with health and safety legislation where client's work activities overlap with the construction work (HSW Act, MHSW Regs, etc)
- Ensure so far as is reasonably practicable, that the principal contractor's health and safety plan is suitable (regulation 10)

**Commissioning and handover:**

- Take such steps as is reasonable for the client to take to keep health and safety file available for inspection (regulation 12(11))

### PLANNING

- If required, be in a position to give adequate advice to client on competence and provision for health and safety by designers (regulation 14(c)(i))
- Ensure, so far as reasonably practicable, designers comply with duties (regulation 14(a))
- Take such steps as is reasonable for the planning supervisor to take to ensure co-operation between designers (regulation 14(b))

**SUPERVISOR**

Where appropriate, take reasonable steps to inform the client of their duties under the CDM Regulations
(**regulation 13(1)**)

Ensure pre-tender stage health and safety plan is prepared
(**regulation 15(1) - (3)**)

Ensure health and safety file is prepared
(**regulation 14(d)**)

If required, be in a position to give adequate advice to client on competence and provision for health and safety by contractors
(**regulation 14(c)(ii)**)

If required, be in a position to give adequate advice to contractors on competence and provision for health and safety by designers
(**regulation 14(c)(i)**)

If required give adequate advice to client on the suitability of the health and safety plan prepared by principal contractor
(**regulation 14(c)(ii)**)

Deliver health and safety file to client
(**regulation 14(f)**)

**DESIGNERS**

Give adequate regard to the hierarchy of risk control when carrying out design work
(**regulation 13(2)(a)**)

Ensure design includes adequate information about health and safety
(**regulation 13(2)(b)**)

Co-operate with the planning supervisor and other designers
(**regulation 13(2)(c)**)

Ensure that when arranging for any designer(s) to prepare a design they are competent and have made adequate provision for health and safety
(**regulations 8(2) and 9(2)**)

Ensure that when arranging for any contractor(s) to carry out or manage construction work, they are competent and have made adequate provision for health and safety
(**regulations 8(3) and 9(3)**)

75

| CONCEPT AND FEASIBILITY | DESIGN AND PLANNING | TENDER/SELECTION STAGE | CONSTRUCTION PHASE | COMMISSIONING AND HANDOVER |
|---|---|---|---|---|
| | | | Ensure health and safety plan is prepared for construction work and is kept up to date (regulation 15(4)) | |
| | | | Take reasonable steps to ensure co-operation between contractors (regulation 16(1)(a)) | |
| | | | Ensure compliance with rules if these are made, take reasonable steps that only authorised people are allowed onto site and display notification form (regulation 16(1)(b) - (d)) | |
| | | | Provide planning supervisor with information relevant to the health and safety file (regulation 16(1)(e)) | |
| | | | May give directions to contractors (regulation 16(2)(a)) | |
| | | | May make rules in the health and safety plan. If they are made, they should be in writing (regulations 16(2)(b) and (3)) | |
| | | | So far as is reasonably practicable, ensure information is provided to contractors (regulation 17(1)) | |
| | | | So far as is reasonably practicable, ensure contractors provide training and information to employees (regulation 17(2)) | |
| | | | Ensure discussions with and advice from people at work and that there are arrangements for the co-ordination of views from people on site (regulation 18) | |

**PRINCIPAL CONTRACTOR**

Ensure that when arranging for any designer(s) to prepare a design they are competent and have made adequate provision for health and safety
(regulations 8(2) and 9(2))

Ensure that when arranging for any contractor(s) to carry out or manage construction work they are competent and have made adequate provision for health and safety
(regulations 8(3) and 9(3))

Co-operate with principal contractor
(regulation 19(1))

Pass to principal contractor information which will affect health and safety, is relevant to the health and safety file or is relevant to RIDDOR
(regulations 19(b), (e) and (f))

Comply with directions of principal contractor and rules in health and safety plan
(regulations 19(c) and (d))

Provide information and training to employees
( HSW Act, MHSW Regulations, etc)

Ensure that when arranging for any designer(s) to prepare a design they are competent and have made adequate provision for health and safety
(regulations 8(2) and 9(2))

Ensure that when arranging for any contractors to carry out or manage construction work they are competent and have made adequate provision for health and safety
(regulations 8(3) and 9(3))

**CONTRACTORS**

77

# Appendix 5

## (Appendix 7 from the HSC "Guide to managing health and safety in construction")

### NOTIFICATION OF A PROJECT — Form 10 (rev)

**A5.01** HSE Health & Safety Executive **Notification of project**

**Note**

1. This form can be used to notify any project covered by the Construction (Design and Management) Regulations 1994 which will last longer than 30 days or 500 person days. It can also be used to provide additional details that were not available at the time of initial notification of such projects. (Any day on which construction work is carried out (including holidays and weekends) should be counted, even if the work on that day is of short duration. A person day is one individual, including supervisors and specialists, carrying out construction work for one normal working shift.)

2. The form should be completed and sent to the HSE area office covering the site where construction work is to take place. You should send it as soon as possible after the planning supervisor is appointed to the project.

3. The form can be used by contractors working for domestic clients. In this case only parts 4-8 and 11 need to be filled in.

**HSE - For official use only**

| Client | V | PV | NV | Planning supervisor | V | PV | NV |
|---|---|---|---|---|---|---|---|
| Focus serial number | | | | Principal contractor | V | PV | NV |

**1** Is this the initial notification of this project or are you providing additional information that was not previously available

Initial notification ☐    Additional notification ☐

**2 Client:** name, full address, postcode and telephone number *(if more than one client, please attach details on separate sheet)*

Name:                                   Telephone number:

Address:

Postcode:

**3 Planning Supervisor:** name, full address, postcode and telephone number

Name:                                   Telephone number:

Address:

Postcode:

**4 Principal Contractor** *(or contractor when project for a domestic client)* name, full address, postcode and telephone number

Name:                                   Telephone number:

Address:

Postcode:

**5 Address of site:** where construction work is to be carried out

Address:

Postcode

F10 (rev 03.95)

**6 Local Authority:** name of the local government district council or island council within whose district the operations are to be carried out

```
┌─────────────────────────────────────────────────────────────────────────┐
│                                                                           │
│                                                                           │
└─────────────────────────────────────────────────────────────────────────┘
```

**7 Please give your estimates on the following:** Please indicate if these estimates are original ☐   revised ☐   *(tick relevant box)*

   a. The planned date for the commencement of the construction work

   b. How long the construction work is expected to take *(in weeks)*

   c. The maximum number of people carrying out construction work on site at any one time

   d. The number of contractors expected to work on site

**8 Construction work:** give brief details of the type of construction work that will be carried out

```
┌─────────────────────────────────────────────────────────────────────────┐
│                                                                           │
│                                                                           │
│                                                                           │
│                                                                           │
└─────────────────────────────────────────────────────────────────────────┘
```

**9 Contractors:** name, full address and postcode of those who have been chosen to work on the project *(if required continue on a separate sheet) .(Note this information is only required when it is known at the time notification is first made to HSE. An update is not required)*

```
┌─────────────────────────────────────────────────────────────────────────┐
│                                                                           │
│                                                                           │
│                                                                           │
│                                                                           │
└─────────────────────────────────────────────────────────────────────────┘
```

**Declaration of planning supervisor**

**10 I hereby declare that** ................................................................................. *(name of organisation)* has been appointed as planning supervisor for the project

  Signed by or on behalf of the organisation ...................................................... *(print name)* .......................................................

  Date ................................................................

**Declaration of principal contractor**

**11 I hereby declare that** ................................................................................. *(name of principal contractor)* has been appointed as principal contractor for the project. *(or contractor undertaking project for domestic client)*

  Signed by or on behalf of the organisation ...................................................... *(print name)* .......................................................

  Date ................................................................

# INDEX

**(All references are to paragraph number)**

570.26 SIM

P942.075
324~2~(942)
~~~~~~ .

247.5586